Fundamental

Included in the series:*

* Also published in French. Other titles to appear.

National and school-based development

Arieh Lewy

Paris 1991
UNESCO: International Institute for Educational Planning

The Swedish International Development Authority (SIDA) has provided financial assistance for the publication of this booklet.

Published in 1991 by the United Nations
Educational, Scientific and Cultural Organization
7 place de Fontenoy, 75700, Paris
Printed in France by Imprimerie Gauthier-Villars, 75018 Paris

Cover design by Bruno Pfäffli
ISBN 92-803-1141-7

Foreword

The booklets in this series are written primarily for two types of clientèle: those engaged in educational planning and administration, in developing as well as developed countries; and others, less specialised, such as senior government officials and policy-makers who seek a more general understanding of educational planning and of how it is related to overall national development. They are intended to be of use either for private study or in formal training programmes.

Since this series was launched in 1967 practices and concepts of educational planning have undergone substantial change. Many of the assumptions which underlay earlier attempts to rationalise the process of educational development have been criticised or abandoned. If rigid mandatory centralised planning has now clearly proven to be inappropriate however, all forms of planning have not been banished. On the contrary the need for collecting data, evaluating the efficiency of existing programmes, undertaking a wide range of studies, exploring the future and fostering broad debate on these bases to guide educational policy- and decision-making has become even more acute than before.

The scope of educational planning has been broadened. In addition to the formal system of education, it is now applied to all other important educational efforts in non-formal settings. Attention to the growth and expansion of educational systems is being complemented and sometimes even replaced by a growing concern for the quality of the entire educational process and for the control of its results. Finally, planners and administrators have become more and more aware of the importance of implementation strategies and of the role of different regulatory mechanisms in this respect: the choice of financing methods, the examination and certification procedures or various other

5

regulation and incentive structures. The concern of planners is twofold : to reach a better understanding of the validity of education in its own empirically observed specific dimensions and to help in defining appropriate strategies for change.

The purposes of these booklets include monitoring the evolution and change in educational policies and their effect upon educational planning requirements; highlighting current issues of educational planning and analysing them in the context of their historical and societal setting; and disseminating methodologies of planning which can be applied in the context of both the developed and the developing countries.

In order to help the Institute identify the real up-to-date issues in educational planning and policy-making in different parts of the world, an Editorial Board has been appointed composed of two general editors and five associate editors from different regions, all professionals of high repute in their field. At the first meeting of this new Editorial Board in January 1990, its members identified key topics to be covered in the coming issues, under the following headings:

1. Education and development.
2. Equity.
3. Quality of education.
4. Structure, administration and management of education.
5. Curriculum.
6. Cost and financing of education.
7. Planning techniques and approaches.
8. Information systems, monitoring and evaluation.

One or two associate editors correspond to each heading.

The series has been carefully planned but no attempt has been made to avoid differences or even contradictions in the views expressed by the authors. The Institute itself does not wish to impose any official doctrine. Thus, while the views are the responsibility of the authors and may not always be shared by UNESCO or the IIEP, they warrant attention in the international forum of ideas. Indeed, one of the purposes of this series is to reflect a diversity of experience and opinions by giving different authors from a wide range of backgrounds and disciplines the opportunity to express their views on changing theories and practices in educational planning.

A very important issue in educational planning and administration nowadays is that of decentralisation and of how much autonomy should be left to regions, communities and institutions. The debate is particularly vivid in the area of curriculum development. What is likely to contribute most to the quality and the relevance of education? A curriculum developed by high level experts at the central level, with the risk of not being implemented, or a curriculum developed at the regional- or school-levels. In order to review current knowledge on this subject, the Editorial Board requested Professor Arieh Lewy of the Tel-Aviv University, Israel, to prepare this booklet on "National and School-Based Curriculum Development". While doing so, Professor Lewy presents a number of very interesting experiences in developed and developing countries. As the author points out, it is clearly not a simple question of either one or the other, but rather a matter of finding the right balance between what is to be defined centrally and what is to be defined locally.

The Institute would like to thank Professor T. Neville Postlethwaite, co-general editor and special editor of this issue, for the active role he played in its preparation.

Jacques Hallak
Director, IIEP

7

8

Preface

What children are expected to learn in school has a major affect on what they do learn. But, who decides what the curriculum should be for all of the children in a school system? Can it be that in large countries where there are different cultures and different types of labour markets in different parts of the country there should be one national curriculum or should it be different for different provinces, regions, or districts? Or, how different should it be?

The planning of what will be taught, the way in which the teaching-learning materials will be produced, the trailing of such materials and their subsequent revision, the implementation of the curriculum involving teacher education and the distribution of materials and, sometimes, accompanying teacher guides is a lengthy task involving many skills.

But, each school is based in a small community. And often, each community can have slightly different needs from other, even neighbouring communities. Should it, therefore, be an individual school which determines its own curriculum?

In short, is it 'better' to have nationally-determined curricula or school-based curricula? As can be imagined, much depends on the meaning of the terms *National Curriculum* and *School-Based Curriculum* and, in the end, both have their place.

Professor Arieh Lewy, a person who has worked in curriculum development and evaluation in many industrialised and developing countries, has taken up these issues in detail in this booklet in the 'Fundamentals of Educational Planning Series.' He has, furthermore, suggested how the 'top-down' and 'bottom-up' modes can be fused.

Apart from providing and maintaining school buildings and equipment and making sure that children attend school, educational planners must ensure a curriculum appropriate to societal as well as individual needs and the training of the teachers to implement it. This booklet will be of direct interest to all planners concerned with improving the quality of education and those dealing with the determination and implementation of curricula in particular.

T. Neville Postlethwaite
Co-general Editor

Contents

Introduction

Traditionally, curriculum was conceived of as the totality of skills and topics to be taught in schools. Quite frequently, the curriculum was determined by age-old traditions, and remained unchanged for long periods of time. Consequently, no need was felt to produce a formal curriculum document, and in the cases in which such a document was produced, it contained a concise list of skills and topics. These were occasionally accompanied by some explanation about their importance, the sequence of their teaching and the time to be allocated to their teaching. Documents of this type have been usually referred to as syllabuses. Since syllabuses were quite stable over several years, and were only altered after long periods of time, educational systems did not need to employ curriculum officials on a permanent basis. The revision of school syllabuses was usually carried out by ad hoc committees.

The *New Curriculum Movement* of the late 1950s brought about changes in the conceptual definition of curriculum, the specification of physical objects through which it was embodied and the way it became produced. Adopting the idea of the 'Structure of Discipline', it employed academic and discipline-oriented criteria for determining what should be taught in schools. The scope of objects considered to constitute the physical embodiment of the curriculum became broadened to contain, in addition to the syllabus, textbooks, workbooks, teachers' guides, demonstration instruments, tests, and so on. To cope with the complex task of preparing a broad variety of curriculum objects, to control their quality, to adapt them to the changing conditions of the environment and the state-of-the-art of disciplines taught in schools, large-scale curriculum development institutions were established across the world by central educational authorities and/or other, publicly supported foundations.

These institutions had hardly succeeded in producing the first set of curricula for all grade levels and subjects taught in schools, when arguments were brought up against such a 'top-down' curriculum development approach, claiming that schools and teachers should play an active role in developing their own curricula (Connelly 1972). In the 1980s a strong counter-movement opposing the views of the New Curriculum Movement emerged. It became known as the *School-Based Curriculum Development* (SBCD) movement (Skilbeck 1984). The operational implications of this movement were not stated with a sufficient level of clarity, and it created some confusion among educational planners. Several questions were raised which have not been seriously considered, let alone satisfactorily answered:

- Do the ideas of the SBCD movement imply that national or centrally operating curriculum development centers should be dismantled?
- Should the scope of their work be reduced drastically?
- Alternatively, should the SBCD supplement centrally developed curricula, while national curriculum development centers continue to fulfil the leading role in supplying curricula for the educational system and in assuming responsibility for promoting supplementary SBCD activities?

The uncertainty about the implications of the SBCD movement has been felt more strongly in emerging educational systems of developing countries, and mainly in those that have not yet established national curriculum development centers and in which a newly established center has not yet completed the work of producing curricula for all grade levels and school subjects.

Should such educational systems establish a curriculum center, or encourage existing curriculum centers to complete the work of producing a national curriculum, or in the face of the ideas of the newly emerging counter-movement, should they delegate the work of curriculum development into the hands of communities, schools and teachers?

This booklet examines issues and problems related to these dilemmas, and summarizes experience accumulated in the last two decades, both in developing and developed countries. It also examines the roles various curriculum developing agencies can successfully carry out and whether there is an adequate relation between these two types of curriculum developing bodies. It is hoped that such information may be of use to educational planners in initiating and monitoring curriculum developing activities.

The first chapter of the booklet provides a historical overview of central and local or school-based curriculum development practices in various countries across the world, and traces changes since the emergence of the New Curriculum Movement of the late 1950s in the conceptions about the role of these two types of curriculum development activities. The second chapter addresses issues related to defining basic terms used in the context of curriculum development and discusses the implications of adopting one or another definition.

Chapter 3 describes varieties of SBCD activities, and demonstrates that the scope of SBCD may vary from minor adaptation at the school level of externally produced curriculum materials, through producing supplementary curriculum units of local interest, to producing alternative and innovative courses for being included in the school programme. Chapter 4 examines the role of various local groups in curriculum development activities, such as the local authorities, the community, local cultural institutions, voluntary organizations, the local business and industry establishments, the school community, the parents and the local higher education and teacher training institutions. It also examines the conditions which are conducive to increasing the success of collaborative enterprises among schools, and between schools and research or development institutions. Chapter 5 deals with the evaluation of SBCD programmes and distinguishes between examining the quality of a particular set of curriculum materials, evaluating the school's success in taking advantage of available local resources for intensifying SBCD activities, and the contribution of SBCD activities in a whole educational system for improving the quality of education and for raising the level of educational outcomes. Chapter 6 summarizes the advantages and disadvantages of SBCD activities.

Finally, the last chapter of the booklet points out the complementary nature of national, and school-based curriculum development and advises educational planners how to get the most out of curriculum development activities of both types.

I. National and school-based curriculum development: a historical perspective

Since the 1950s large-scale curriculum reforms have been introduced in most educational systems across the world. The first and most notable among them was the curriculum reform of the 1950s in the United States of America. Other educational systems followed suit later and initiated educational reforms of a similar type. In the USA the reforms fed on severe criticism of what was taught in schools. Leading science experts in American universities asserted that the 'soft pedagogy' of American education, by emphasizing the idea of life adjustment and supporting the inclusion in the school programme of non-academic activities, such as social dancing and peer-group relations, reduced the motivation of youngsters to take advanced courses in science and to strive for excellence in scholarly achievement. In other countries, which had not experimented with 'soft pedagogies' dissatisfaction was also expressed about the science curricula whose content had been watered down and which lacked academic rigour. Consequently, it was asserted that such courses failed to prepare secondary school students for challenging science courses at the universities.

Such criticism reached larger audiences, and those who were concerned with the advancement of science and technology argued for an overall revision of science and mathematics curricula in both the primary and the secondary school. Scientists of renown, first in the USA, and a few years later in other industrialized countries, took the lead in developing new curricula. In contrast to previous curricula, which either imparted functional knowledge such as carrying out everyday mathematical operations or balancing a cheque book or containing a heavy load of factual information, the new curricula aimed at providing an up-to-date and scientifically valid picture of a particular discipline. They emphasized the key concepts and broad ideas underlying the structure of the discipline and focused on teaching inquiry methods which aimed at the generation of new knowledge as well as the acquisition of existing knowledge. Laboratory activities served as a means of discovery rather than of verification, and in this way added to the excitement of the scientist's work. The activities involved in producing innovative curricula of this type became referred to in the curriculum literature as the New Curriculum Movement.

Some basic ideas of this movement were shared by curriculum developers in the USA and the United Kingdom, but due to historical differences between these two countries in the approach towards producing curricula they developed different definitions of the curriculum user. In the USA the curriculum developers provided textbooks for learners, while in the United Kingdom they produced teachers guides instructing teachers what and how to teach their classes.

The development of such innovative programmes gained massive financial support in the USA from the National Science Foundation, and in the United Kingdom the Nuffield Foundation provided financial backing. Some developing countries also revealed interest in the ideas of the New Curriculum Movement and hurried either to adapt foreign programmes for local use or to establish National Curriculum Centers that developed new programmes adopting the operational patterns of curriculum development teams in industrialized countries. Large-scale curriculum development projects were initiated in various countries in the 1960s and the 1970s, although by then the general enthusiasm for such programmes was abating.

Beyond the innovative pedagogical ideas described above, these programmes were characterized by common development and dissemination procedures. The programmes were prepared by professional teams, mostly led by subject specialists of high reputation. As indicated above, the recipients of the new programmes in the USA were the students, and in the United Kingdom the teachers. In both countries the development teams were engaged in intensive work for long periods (usually one to three years) before the first sets of instructional material were released for use. Before release each component of the programme was tried out in schools, meticulously evaluated, and revised on the basis of the evaluation results. Dissemination of the programme was in a 'top down' manner. The development teams undertook extensive in-service training of teachers to prepare them for using the new programmes adequately. Teachers were required to fulfil the role of mediators between the new set of instructional material and the pupils; their task was to carry out activities specified in teachers guides or in textbooks.

In many cases the 'center-periphery' approach to dissemination was employed: the producers of the innovative programmes, who usually themselves were or represented the owners, established regional offices equipped with centrally provided guidelines and directives to help teachers overcome difficulties encountered in operating the programme. It is of interest to note that these large-scale curriculum projects originated in countries where centralized school systems did not prevail. In the USA and the United Kingdom, at the projects initiation, the curriculum was considered to be the prerogative of the school, and schools were keen to avoid external intervention in matters which they considered to pertain to the domain of their autonomy.

As it turned out, the innovative programmes were judged superior to their predecessors. Critics thought them interesting, even exciting, and the lessons focused on significant aspects of the discipline. Empirical studies have shown that the programme assignment for students, if well presented, has high appeal for the users. Teachers received well assembled kits of accessories, obviating the need to search for their own auxiliary course material. Full use was made of colour and artwork in books and other materials. High-tech enrichment materials were also produced, importing communication techniques from the advertising and leisure industries and presenting an exciting new world.

In spite of this, these new curricula reached a surprisingly small proportion of schools. As reported by Harlen (1985), attempts to introduce active inquiry based science into primary schools yielded disappointing results. She indicated that in the United Kingdom in the middle of the 1970s half of the primary classes had no science in the curriculum, and only about 10 per cent of the schools had developed science programmes seriously. Similarly and at the same time, in the USA about 85 per cent of schools did not use the materials of the major curriculum projects.

Leading curriculum experts tried to explain why costly programmes developed by the nation's experts with much financial support and with books and instructional materials of high quality, failed to gain a foothold in the schools. Some claimed that the new programmes required teachers to assume new roles in the class, and that the teachers were not well prepared for them. The new programmes encouraged the asking of questions which could be answered only by joint inquiry of teachers and pupils; the teacher was no longer the source of knowledge, while pupils frequently would be in possession of relevant knowledge that the teacher did not have. Others claimed that some teachers may have had a weak background in science and consequently lacked the confidence to handle science at such an advanced level; that they moreover lacked a commitment to science instruction as an indispensable component of primary education, and for such reasons avoided the use of these innovative programmes. Indeed even in secondary schools intensive science study based on active learning, problem solving, and inquiry was required only for those who opted to specialize in science. Others were allowed to content themselves with taking an introductory course imparting knowledge of a factual type.

These explanations imply an optimistic view of centralized curricula disseminated through a center-periphery mechanism. They imply that optimal use of the programmes may be achieved by better preparation of teachers through pre-service or in-service courses and by convincing the educational authorities, parents, school boards and curriculum committee members of the value of these programmes.

In the 1980s, however, the failure of large-scale central curricula was identified by some critics as the result of the inherent characteristics of curriculum centralism, rather than being caused by shortcomings in implementation. They claimed that experts operating at development centers far from the users of their products were not in a position to transmit the subtle innovative features of new programmes to teachers with whom they had no personal contact, nor were they able to motivate teachers to change their teaching habits to the extent needed to ensure the success of the new curricula. In this view, only grassroots initiatives had a chance of succeeding, and accordingly teachers were invited to participate actively in developing their own curricula.

Another consideration of the proponents of this view was that the professional status of the teachers would be enhanced if, instead of serving as obedient implementers of externally imposed curricula, they were empowered to make decisions about what to teach and given the challenge of participating in the creative process of producing new instructional materials. Furthermore, the idea of self-determination and the importance of local autonomy, suited the democratic ethos better than the traditional demand of compliance with externally imposed regulations.

The widespread perception of the inherent weaknesses of central curricula led in the 1970s and 1980s to the rise of a counter movement which became known as *School-Based Curriculum Development* (SBCD). This emerging curriculum movement rejected the operational principles and partly also the ideals of the New Curriculum Movement, which in the 1950s and 1960s had hoped to institute worldwide reform in schools. The School-Based Curriculum Development differed from its rival, the New Curriculum Movement, on the questions of where curricula should be developed (at central offices or at the school level) and who should be involved in making decisions (national experts or school related persons); it was also opposed to the rigid division between subject areas, favouring instead an interdisciplinary approach for topics which required it, and linking curriculum to the learner's immediate environment and personal experience. The name School-Based Curriculum Development conveyed principally that

21

the shortcomings of the New Curriculum Movement were to be remedied by having curriculum-related decisions made at school level.

In emerging educational systems of the Third World priority was given to establishing a national curriculum that was expected to strengthen national identity, contribute to modernization of the educational system and hasten provision of, at least, primary education for all. The idea of national unity gained greater emphasis than that of respect for divergent values and interests within the nation. Educational planners believed that national goals were best achieved through central planning, and therefore did not press for greater autonomy on the schools' behalf, on matters of curriculum. The majority of initiatives in this area is consequently based on voluntary co-operation among groups of schools.

Nevertheless, in the 1980s, first those developing countries which had already succeeded in producing a national curriculum, and later also those which failed to accomplish this task, became aware of the desirability of encouraging curriculum-related initiatives at regional, local and school levels, in part to supplement the national curriculum and in part to substitute some of its elements.

These two patterns of curriculum development, the centralized and the school-based approaches, are not innovations of the second half of the 20th century. Both of them have existed for a long time. The central curriculum development has a long history in France and Germany. In France the study plans of the *Ancient Régime* were replaced by new programmes of studies between 1821 and 1840. These programmes specified the range of topics for which candidates could be examined nationally. Every school in France was provided with an identical programme and timetable. The programme each year was the continuation of the previous year's work, the pupil being introduced to ever more complex ideas. To move up from one class to the next, pupils had to show mastery of the previous year's programme. Such a restrictive course of schoolwork left little latitude to teachers and hardly took account of the personality of either the class or individual pupils.

Germany also has a tradition of centralized curricula. Prussia started to issue detailed study plans for its schools in the 18th century, a process completed at the beginning of the 19th century. This was described as the first formal curriculum 'in the modern sense' of an educational system. It comprised the specification of compulsory subjects accompanied by their respective number of hours (timetable), stipulations on the aims, content and method of teaching and compulsory reading assignments. To some extent the Prussian curriculum also stipulated the requirements for promotion from class-to-class and for obtaining certificates (Menck 1989).

In contrast to these two instances of highly centralized curricula, in the USA and the United Kingdom full authority for curriculum decisions was delegated to the local authorities and they empowered schools to exercise autonomy in matters of curriculum. At the beginning of the century, in the USA, more than 100,000 independent school districts operated, each of them having full power to make curricular decisions. The number of school districts was then substantially reduced and toward the end of the 1980s there were only approximately 16,000 school districts in the whole country. Even so, the American educational system had 16,000 different school curricula.

England and Wales, making up the largest educational system in the United Kingdom, have an old tradition of decentralized, school-based curriculum. During the long history of these political units the central authorities have intervened very little in curricular matters of the curriculum. Some curricular specifications for primary schools issued in 1862 were abolished in 1926, and those issued for secondary schools in 1902 were abolished in 1944. After the passing of the 1944 Educational Act there was no national specification of the curriculum in England and Wales apart from the obligation for all schools to provide religious education. For the entire period from 1944 to 1988, when the government's proposal for a National Curriculum for England and Wales, incorporated in the Education Reform Act, received royal assent, school-based curriculum development was the rule.

Examining the two hundred year long history of these conflicting patterns of curriculum development we note that no single pattern was fully dominant in any of the above-mentioned countries. As Goldhammer (1985) remarked: "in spite of its highly centralised governance over primary and secondary schools France has a long tradition of local involvement (in school matters)". [p.2060]

At the same time one should be aware that the school's freedom in curricular matters has its limits. Dealing with the educational system in England and Wales, Skilbeck (1984) notes:

"The freedom of the school also entails the exercise of their prerogatives and responsibilities, by the several legitimate interests over and above the teachers (e.g. parents, students, community groups, local and central government)". [Skilbeck p.86]

There are also other constraints, such as external examinations, job requirements, and legal considerations, for example, the obligation in the 1944 Act to provide religious education.

The above examples support the view that, in practice, schools cannot and do not rigidly follow programmes prescribed by external or central authorities, but that, at the same time, the school cannot disregard externally imposed constraints in deciding what to teach.

Implications

1. The history of curriculum changes in any particular educational system has implications for educational planning, and therefore it should be thoroughly studied by curriculum developers.

2. Even in a country with a relatively short history of maintaining a modern educational system, it is highly important to be aware of the changes which occurred in the school programme, of the roots of the present day curriculum, and of the consequences of the national educational heritage.

3. It is equally important to study trends in school programmes across the world.

4. Curricular decisions have to be made, and are made, both at national and local level. At no one of these two levels alone can all parameters of the school programme be determined.

5. The distribution of decision-making power between the national and local level authorities changes over time. In implementing such changes, attention should be paid to the traditions of educational planning in the country, and in most cases it is desirable that such changes be incremental rather than radical.

6. In emergent educational systems, priority should be given to producing a national curriculum framework. Local level curriculum decisions should deal with supplementing the national framework and adapting it to local conditions.

II. The meaning of 'school-based curriculum development'

Conflicting views about the advantages and disadvantages of centralistic and school-based curriculum development practice have been intensified by differences in defining the component elements of the complex term 'school-based curriculum development'. Therefore, before dealing with the substantial issues of curriculum development, an attempt will be made to provide a working definition of the terms used.

Curriculum

As noticed by several writers, the term curriculum is elusive and epistemologically ill-defined. There is little agreement on where curriculum matters end and the rest of education begins. Not surprisingly, there are many definitions of curriculum. Rule (1973) identified 119 definitions of the term, and there have been several additions to this list since then.

The ambiguity of the term is intensified by the fact that in most European languages there is no equivalent to the English 'curriculum'. In French there is the term 'programme scolaire', in German 'Lehrplan', and in Russian 'soderzhanie obrazovaniya'. These terms tend to correspond to the English 'syllabus'. A Russian scholar questioning the meaning of the term curriculum said that he was unable to see exactly what English-speaking scholars understood by the word, and he urged them to define it as the theory of programmes of instruction (Muckle 1988). This narrow definition is adopted by several American experts too. Good (1973, 3rd edition), for example, defines curriculum as "a general overall plan of the content, or specific materials of instruction that the school should offer the student by way of

qualifying him for graduation or certification or for entrance into a professional or vocational field" (p.157). Taba's (1962) definition of curriculum is "a plan for learning" (p.9). This is broader than Good's definition: "plan for learning" means more than 'a plan of content' inasmuch as it must comprise instructional materials, as well as the outline of the content units. Indeed, in the 1960s curriculum experts produced curriculum packages containing -- in addition to the traditional textbook, worksheets and teachers guide -- demonstration charts, study enrichment materials, equipment and materials for carrying out experiments and audiovisual teaching aids (such as film clips and video cassettes, which later were substituted by video-discs) supplemented by interactive computer programmes. Nevertheless, both of these definitions refer to physical objects such as documents, books and instructional material, and thus foster an undesirable dualism. As indicated by Portelli (1987), the emphasis on what should be taught tends to neglect the learner. From the 1930s onwards the curriculum has often been defined in terms of experience in order to eliminate this dualism. The Tyler-rationale regards 'learning experiences' as a crucial element of the curriculum (Tyler 1950). Macdonald (1986; p. 207) stresses 'learning experiences' saying that curriculum is not the course to be run, but the course that was run. The tendency to define curriculum as an experience, and not merely as a plan, arose not only to avoid the undesirable dualism between a written document and what is going on in the school, but also in response to the growing feeling that most of the products of the curriculum development efforts of the 1960s and 1970s were not put into practice. The distinction between plan and experience was analytically studied by Goodlad and Klein (1979). Their study allowed to define the following curriculum phases:
1.   Intended curriculum, or curriculum plan and outline, usually referred to as syllabus.
2.   Instructional materials to be used by teachers and learners in realizing this plan.
3.   Teaching learning activities initiated and carried out in the class.   These activities are not necessarily identical with those specified in the materials provided.   Some activities may be

omitted from the actual programme, substituted by new ones or they may be modified.

4. The learners' personal experiences, which again may be related only to a subset of activities carried out in the class. A learner may be inattentive during a particular activity in the class, or may not grasp, or may misinterpret, a particular event in the class.

5. The outcome of using the curriculum, or the level of mastery of curricular objectives attained by learners.

When considering the debate between central and school-based curriculum development it is of interest to note that the phases described above also represent a continuum of diminishing levels of universality. A syllabus or a curricular plan may be common to a large group of schools or even to a whole educational system. Several different series of textbooks may be produced on the basis of a single syllabus. Indeed, in most centraled educational systems, where a common syllabus of studies is prescribed for schools of a particular type, the educational authorities encourage the use, or even support the production, of several sets of competing instructional materials, provided each of them follows the syllabus.

What is described above as the third phase of the curriculum is, by definition, school-based, since it is unique for each teacher or class. The last two phases are unique to each individual. In other words, focusing on the fourth and fifth phases of curriculum, as defined by Goodlad and Klein (1970), two persons attending the same class may well seem to have encountered two different curricula.

Development

It is easier to define 'development' than 'curriculum'. Development is usually not used as a technical term, although in several areas, such as geometry, mathematics, photography and music, it has a particular technical denotation. Among the definitions appearing in the Oxford English Dictionary, "a fuller disclosure or working out of the details of anything, as a plan, a scheme, a plot of a novel" comes closest to the meaning suggested to the expression 'curriculum development'. According to this definition the preparation of the plan would not constitute a part of development, but only the elaboration of the plan or putting it into practice. In ordinary usage, however, development may refer to preparing a plan as well as working out its details.

Thus, curriculum development may refer to preparing a plan of operation for putting into use an existing syllabus, including the selection of textbooks and instructional materials, or it may mean producing a syllabus and the accessories needed for using it in the class. In particular, it may mean the writing of textbooks, teachers guides and the preparation of teaching aids, and in some cases also the evaluation instruments for examining the attainment of the programme goals. Moreover, all activities related to establishing the validity or the adequacy of both plan and accessories may legitimately be described as curriculum development activities. Thus, curriculum development activities may begin with the preparation of a syllabus, but quite often they start at a phase when the syllabus is already available.

Braybrooke and Lindblom (1963) distinguished between two types of curriculum development actions. The first strives to develop a comprehensively reformed curriculum, in which all elements of the programme are developed anew without relying on elements of the available programme. The second works according to the 'disjointed incremental' pattern, changing only small, selected elements of the existing programme.

Reference to two types of curriculum development is also made by Connelly (1972). He distinguishes between 'local-user development' and 'external development'. The *first* refers to development activities carried out by the users of the curriculum and the *second* to the development of the curriculum components by others. Elaborating on this distinction Connelly argues that, in theory, a curriculum can be fully developed either by the users or by external developers, although such cases rarely occur in practice. Most frequently, local users will participate in development activities, but they will also take advantage of curriculum components developed by external developers, such as research and development institutions or commercial agencies.

According to Connelly's view, the curriculum implemented in the class almost always contains a locally developed component. Only on rare occasions, as when teachers introduce into their classes a set of externally prepared, programmed instructional materials and create an environment of self-instruction, is the teaching-learning fully dependent on an externally developed curriculum. Even so, this type of instruction constitutes only one part of the overall learning activities of the class.

Silberstein (1979) elaborates on Connelly's ideas. He uses Connellys distinction between development activities of curriculum users and of external groups and agrees that the process of curriculum development should be viewed as a continuum beginning with the work of a central body, external to the school, and ending in teaching-learning situations in the classroom, but he does not accept the sharp differentiation of roles attributed by Connelly to these two types of developers. A schematic representation of Connelly's view is presented in *Figure 2.1*.

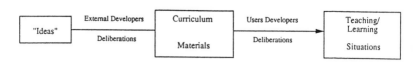

Figure 2.1 Curriculum development: one continuum

According to this scheme, curriculum development is a two phase process, in which the first group of actors finishes its role with the completion of the first phase, upon which, at the second stage, a new group of actors appears on the scene phase. The 'external' developers and the user developers each work on a different part of the curriculum development continuum, and the work of the 'user' developers begins where the former leave off. According to Connelly, the ideal 'user' developer can be described metaphorically as a customer in a supermarket. On the shelves are tins with labels specifying the contents, the ingredients, and various dishes that can be prepared from the contents. Skilled and intelligent shoppers will select suitable items and will return home and prepare a meal matched to their needs. Similarly, curriculum materials developed by 'external' parties should present clearly 'labelled' alternatives (various viewpoints on teaching the discipline, on psychological and social attitudes, etc.), with specifications of the contents, characteristics (including the theoretical assumptions underlying the curriculum materials), and potential uses of the materials. Intelligent teacher consumers, skilled in the art of selection, will choose the materials they judge suitable, and will alter, augment, process, and transform them to suit their classes.

Silberstein challenges Connelly's linear, two-phase conception, and suggests a model of collaboration between external and user developers as presented in *Figure 2.2*.

According to Silberstein, during the first phase of the process, external developers assume the task of producing the instructional materials. Their involvement in the curriculum process, however, does not come to an end when they have done this, and in the second phase of using the curriculum and implementing it in schools, the external development team has to establish a collaborative relationship with the users and help them continue the work of development. Silberstein lists three further tasks to be undertaken personally by external developers:

- Involvement in work with teacher educators.
- Workshops for developing personalized or localized supplementary curriculum units.
- Workshop for curriculum adaptation.

31

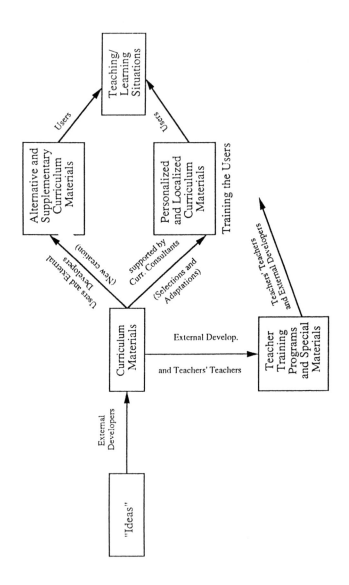

Figure 2.2 Curriculum development: collaborative model

School-based

The expression 'school-based' in the term school-based curriculum development is also interpreted in various ways. Connelly (1972) avoided the expression and substituted 'user-developer'. While these two expressions often have the same meaning and may refer to the same person, i.e. the classroom teacher, this is by no means always the case. A 'user-developer' is not necessarily school-based, and 'school-based' is not necessarily the same as 'user-developer'. The expression 'user-developer' may refer to a team of teachers from various schools working under the guidance of an external curriculum consultant to adapt a set of commercially disseminated instructional materials to the needs of their students. Participation in such a team may take place within the framework of a university-maintained in-service training programme, to which teachers may register on their own initiative and on an individual basis. By using instructional materials developed by the team, a teacher participating in the in-service programme becomes a user-developer, but the programme used by the teacher is not school-based. It was not initiated by the school and it may well be that it was not adopted by other teachers teaching the same subject in parallel classes. If, on the other hand, a school adopts a programme produced or revised by a team of its own teachers, then the programme is school-based, but those teachers who did not participate in its development are not user-developers.

One may also ask who participates in the development of school-based programmes? All the teachers teaching a particular subject? Some of the teachers only? If in a certain school, within the framework imposed by an external authority or by the school authorities, the teachers enjoy a relatively high level of autonomy in determining what to teach and what kind of instructional materials to use, does such a situation represent school-based curriculum development?

As indicated by Sabar (1989):

"...school-based curriculum development ought not to be, and indeed cannot be, reduced to teacher-based curriculum development, important as teachers' roles are at every stage. It should be participatory, that is decisions should be shared with all those involved in the educational experience." (p.202)

Sabar lists several potentially legitimate partners in school-based curriculum development: parents, if possible learners themselves, other institutions and agencies in the society.

Frequently, in educational practice, representatives of the local authorities or of the local educational authorities participate in curriculum decisions. A variety of interest groups such as churches, labour unions, universities and other institutions of higher education, as well as industrial and commercial chambers, claim a say in the school curriculum. Quite often, local authorities prescribe the school programme for all schools in the geographic area of their jurisdiction. Certainly, such arrangements do not represent instances of school-based curriculum development. In the curriculum literature, devolution of power in matters of the curriculum and school-based curriculum development are treated quite often under one heading, while in practice these are two different phenomena. Devolution is a precondition of school-based curriculum development: it may precipitate school-based curriculum development, but it does not in itself constitute a sufficient condition. Without full awareness of the differences between the concepts of devolution, user-developer, and school-based curriculum development statements made about curriculum development may remain void of exact meaning.

The scope of SBCD

The broadest definition of SBCD implies not only full autonomy for the school to decide what to teach, but also a commitment on its behalf to prepare instructional materials for the courses offered, with a minimal reliance on available textbooks. The narrowest definition of SBCD would stipulate that the central educational authorities delegate some freedom to, or bestow some autonomy upon the local or the school authorities in determining a certain part of the school programme.

In practice, we never encounter a full realization of the broadest definition of SBCD. There are no schools which

34

operate according to the principles represented by this broadest definition. On the other hand, employing the narrowest definition, one may say that all schools incorporate some elements of SBCD approach in their routine activities.

The subsequent sections describe SBCD activities which have a substantial impact on life in the school.

Implications

1. Meaningful communication about SBCD is possible only if the terms of the discourse are precisely defined. Consequently, deliberation about curriculum should start with defining the terms used.
2. Contradictory statements and recommendations about SBCD may reflect differences in definitions of terms and, therefore, when used in decision-making context, they must be analyzed with regard to meanings originally attributed to them.
3. Precise definition of terms may lead towards identification of areas of consensus which, in turn, may create a favourable climate for negotiating.

III. Types of school-based curriculum development activities

Some national curriculum frameworks are highly prescriptive. Sometimes they specify educational aims, instructional objectives, curriculum contents and grade level attainment standards. Frequently they also contain a list of approved textbooks, or they are periodically supplemented by such a list. In other countries they provide a loose framework and encourage curriculum development initiatives at a local and school level.

Even the highly prescriptive frameworks bestow a certain autonomy upon the schools in matters of the curriculum. Paradoxically, they frequently oblige schools to exercise autonomy, and to make decisions at the local or school level about a certain part of the curriculum. The scope of school-based decisions about the curriculum varies across countries and across schools within a country, involving mostly from 10 to 30 per cent of the total school programme.

Schools also differ with regard to the types of the programmes they decide to introduce within the framework of the autonomy bestowed upon them. Some schools opt to extend study time for the regular curricular subjects while others introduce topics of local interest, or cross-disciplinary studies related to a particular topic of interest.

Curriculum development at local and school level consists of the following activities: selecting and adapting existing educational programmes, integrating study topics from cognate disciplines into a single course or examining a certain phenomenon or problem through an interdisciplinary or cross-disciplinary approach, and producing new instructional units either for supplementing existing curriculum materials or for creating new learning units.

Selecting curriculum at the school and class levels

The most common curriculum-related decision at the school and class levels consists of selection. In many educational systems the teachers involvement in curriculum development is limited to this act of selection. Moreover, even in those systems where teachers do enjoy a high level of autonomy, curriculum development still means selecting and organizing content units for teaching, and/or selecting appropriate learning materials from those available on the market. The act of selection enables the teacher to play an active role in determining what to teach.

Selection may be regarded as less professionally demanding than producing new curriculum materials, but one should not underestimate the expertise needed for fulfilling this role. By analogy, the professional knowledge required for producing a well written critique about a musical performance is by no means inferior to, though evidently very different from, that needed for playing an instrument and producing enjoyable music.

It should be noted that the right to select is a necessary, but not a sufficient condition, for taking advantage of this privilege. There is also a need for having alternatives to select from. In countries where the production of curriculum materials is a commercial enterprise, the market offers a broad repertoire of such alternatives. Under such circumstances users have to select. In contrast, in countries where the central authorities specify all parameters of the curriculum materials, or even produce them, frequently, there are no alternatives. Consequently, users do not face the difficulties of selection. In developed countries one may observe great competition for customers, and it is not uncommon for a single company to produce alternative versions of a programme to cater for differential needs and tastes in the target population. Thus, for example, the Biological Science Curriculum Study (BSCS) produced three alternative versions of their programme. These became known as the Blue, Green, and Yellow version of the programme. The Blue version of the programme focused on biology at the molecular level, the Green version on populations and communities, while the Yellow version put great emphasis on the cellular level. The user who decided to adopt the BSCS curriculum had to select one of these versions, and was in need of criteria to guide this selection. Developing countries which chose to use the BSCS programme adapted for local use only one of these versions, and thus both the need and the possibility of being engaged in selection was eliminated at an early stage.

Due to scarcity of resources as well as of experts in most developing countries, the scope of alternative sets of curricula and instructional materials is quite limited. Nevertheless, one may identify some attempts of producing alternative sets of textbooks for a single syllabus. Thus, for example, in Botswana in 1989 a new Integrated Social Studies programme for Junior High School was approved by the Social Studies panel of the Department of Education, and almost simultaneously two parallel sets of textbooks were produced: Botswana Social Studies and Junior Secondary Social Studies (Clarken 1990). The users of the programme have the right and the onus to choose between them.

Selecting something which may have significant and long-lasting effect on the life of others requires a reasonable level of connoisseurship. Consequently, teachers need to acquire expertise in selecting curricula, to nurture it, and to use it in their daily work for the benefit of their students.

Selection, in dealing with the curriculum of a school or a class, takes place at various levels. The most comprehensive form of selection is selecting subjects for inclusion in the programme. Most school systems offer a list of elective subjects from which schools have to select the few they will offer. Frequently the central educational authorities prescribe certain rules for selection, like the obligation to select some subject in the field of art or science. Schools may have the right to include in their programme a subject which does not appear in the basic repertoire of elective subjects like archaeology, philosophy of science, etc.

Deciding to use a particular textbook or a particular set of accessories represents another level of curriculum related selection. Also in daily teaching routine the decision by the teacher to deal with one particular exercise in the textbook and skip over another is an instance of determining the parameters of the curriculum through selection.

To prepare teachers for making selections, which best serve the needs of all interested parties, teacher education has to provide basic knowledge and practice in this field.

In practice, one may observe a variety of approaches to selection. The naive consumer may operate according to the principle of 'first seen, first chosen'. The more choosy customer may search till he or she finds a satisfactory object. The hesitant customer may examine a variety of options, and, reaching a level of fatigue, will select the last encountered. The rational decision-maker follows a well-structured, multi-phased method which consists of listing the items on the available repertoire, determining criteria for selection, applying these and rating the items on the repertoire according to the relevant criteria, and finally combining these ratings into a decision-making formula.

Listing the items: In numerous educational systems a great variety of alternative curriculum items is available and the teacher may encounter difficulties when compiling a satisfactory list of alternatives. Frequently, central educational authorities do a preliminary screening and they publish a list of books, or other types of curriculum materials which are approved for use in the school. In other cases, commercial companies or consumer organizations prepare lists which may be used by teachers. Whenever such orientation materials are not readily available, they should be produced locally at the school level or through the co-operation of several schools.

Specifying relevant criteria: The curriculum literature abounds in checklists which specify criteria for selecting curricula, textbooks and other types of curriculum materials. The most comprehensive collection of relevant forms and checklists was compiled by Woodbury (1979). An example of a form provided by Woodbury is presented in *Table 3.1.*

Table 3.1 Curriculum-selection form

		Check one				
Name of Textbook: _____ Grade: _____ Date: _____ Publisher: _____ Reviewer: _____ Author: _____ School _____	Excellent	Good	Fair	Poor	No Opinion	Category Scores*

A. Racism and Sexism: Group 1
 1. Illustrations (examples)
    a. stereotypes
    b. lifestyle
    c. tokenism						

2. Storyline
    a. relationships
    b. standard for success
    c. viewpoint
    d. sexism						

B. Authenticity 1. Accuracy of Facts/ Appropriate to Context						
2. Impartiality of presentation						
3. Up-to-date Information						
C. Appropriateness 1. Contribution to the program objectives						
2. Vocabulary level						
D. Scope 1. Coverage of subject matter						
2. Concept development						

3. Skills development
    (map-reading, use of
    graphs, etc.)						

4. Process development (e.g., problem solving)						
E. Interest 1. Relationship to user's experience						
2. Intellectual challenge						
3. Appeal to students						
F. Organization 1. Sequential development of concepts						
2. Match with District sequences						

TOTAL SCORE = _____

POSSIBLE RANGE =

Source: Woodbury, M. 1979. *Selecting materials for instruction: issues and policies*, Littletown: Libraries Unlimited, p.217.

Armbruster and Anderson (1981) provided a conceptual framework for dealing with textbook-related criteria. They introduced the concept 'considerate text' and defined it as one that incorporates concern for:
(a) Structure (has a discourse structure that best conveys the information).
(b) Coherence (makes the relationships among ideas clear enough so that there is a logical connection from one idea to the next).
(c) Unity (addresses one purpose at a time); and
(d) Audience appropriateness (fits the knowledge base of the reader).

Textbook Evaluation forms for students and teachers have been produced in developing countries, too. Systematic work in this has been done by the *National Council of Educational Research and Training* (NCERT) in New Delhi, India. India has a long tradition of concern for the quality of textbooks, and a series of publications in the 1970s about evaluating textbooks merits international attention. Exemplary questions from the Evaluation Form for Textbooks in English are presented in *Table 3.2.*

Combining the ratings: Finally there is a need to combine the ratings into an overall evaluative statement. The form in table 3.1 suggests a mode of quantitative summary, but one may use qualitative summary based on analytical combination of qualifications or on a holistic-impressionistic judgement.

In rating the quality of any type of instructional materials one should consider the specific needs of a particular group of users. A curriculum or a textbook which serves well one group of learners or teachers may be unsuitable for another group of learners.

Adaptation

Curriculum adaptation is defined by Grobman and Blum (1985) as the modification of a course of study for groups different from those for whom the course was originally prepared. Adaptation can take place at national or system level. It may also take place at school or class level, whenever a teacher or a group

41

of teachers decide to modify some elements of a curriculum used in the school(s).

Table 3.2. Selected items from the questionnaire for textbooks in English

Principles and aspects	Evaluative criteria Criteria
Aims and purposes	• General objectives were developed keeping in view national goals as defined by various Education Commissions. • Specific objectives for different stages were developed, keeping in view time allotted in the syllabus
Content: Linguistic	• The selection of vocabulary is appropriate in terms of frequency based on contemporary spoken and written English of everyday use.
Thematic	• The themes are varied enough in content and form to grip and sustain the interest of children.
Gradation	• Linguistic elements are grouped into stages according to age, grade and maturity level of the children.
Illustrations	• They are relevant and significant to the theme. • They clarify and interpret the verbal content. • They are technically perfect in terms of size, details, colour and print.
Exercises	• They cover all objectives. • They are different types, like essays, and short, controlled composition.

Adaptation at national level consists of changes needed because of differences of an ecological and socio-cultural nature, in historical and political perspectives, or in classroom situations. An example of a system level adaptation is the case of the BSCS (Biological Science Curriculum Study) which was developed in the USA in the 1960s, and which was adapted for use in more than 40 nations and translated into 21 languages.

The need to adapt biology textbooks to local, environmental conditions is emphasized by Grobman and Blum (1985). They provide the following justification:

"Discussions of plants and animals from the local environment make textual materials more relevant for students. Thus for students in the United Kingdom and most of the USA, references to oak, willow, or pine trees would be familiar, but for students in tropical areas of India or the Philippines, they would not. In an adaptation, those examples might be replaced with palm, banana, and banyan trees. In Japan the silkworm is used for many of the genetic experiments for which the fruit fly is employed in the United States". (p.1136)

A close examination of curricula which were transferred from one society to another reveals that adaptation touched not only on issues related to the characteristics of the eco-system, but also on societal features like internalized national attitudes to politics and religion, which are also important factors to be considered in curriculum adaptation (Holmes 1977). Indeed, in the Russian BSCS adaptation, the achievements of Russian scientists were emphasized compared to the original American version, and in the Italian adaptation of the Harvard Physics Project, Galileo is given more space than in the American original.

Other reasons for adapting a curriculum when transferring it from one nation to another may be the differences in available resources for teaching the subject, in terms of time allocation, budget available for sophisticated laboratory equipment, class size, etc.

Even within one single country, regional differences may necessitate adapting a curriculum used in one region of the country to another which is different from the first. A curriculum intended for a highly industrialized region needs adaptation when put to use in a less industrialized, agricultural economy area. Moreover, even transferring to another industrial area, which differs from the previous one with regard to the sources of energy used, raw materials and products, may need modification. Similarly, the transfer of a curriculum prepared for one particular agricultural area to another which grows different crops can be facilitated by making adequate modifications of some learning experiences contained in the programme.

Linguistic or ethnic heterogeneity of a country's population, or parallel maintenance of various school types or school systems inside one region, such as public and religious schools, or vocational and academically oriented secondary schools, may also require adapted versions of an available curriculum.

Adaptation at system level is usually carried out by centrally operating teams of curriculum experts with or without the participation of a few selected teachers.

Curriculum adaptation also takes place at the school and class level, and work of this nature is mostly carried out by teachers who are going to use the adapted materials themselves. Berliner (1982) demonstrated that teachers adapt the goals, objectives, and content of formal curricula to their specific classroom context. They take the freedom to deviate from the mandated programme and modify it by additions, deletions and changes in sequence and emphasis.

Holmes (1989) discussed ethical considerations in the teachers modifying of the curriculum. He argued that, in a free, multi-cultural and individualistic society, both teachers and students may face situations which will require modifying curriculum plans prepared by others.

The modifications carried out at both national and school level may touch upon various aspects of the curriculum. In extreme cases, the adaptation may require minor modifications only, such as changing some illustrations like human figures and/or their dress, types of houses or other dwelling facilities. Such minimal changes will allow the transfer of the curriculum from one group to another. But most frequently, more substantial changes are required for successful curriculum transfer. Blum *et al.* (1981) identified 40 curriculum aspects of which should be considered when a decision about adaptation is made. He grouped them under the following headings: (a) aims; (b) content selection, (c) content organization; (d) learning experiences; and (e) resource materials.

Examples of curriculum adaptation can be found both in developing and in developed countries. As was already mentioned above, the American BSCS programme was adapted for use in, among other countries, Australia, Italy and Russia. In several cases the adaptation also implied translation to another language. The Caribbean version of the BSCS, and the Malaysian adaptation of the Scottish Integrated Science (SIS) programme are interesting examples of curriculum adaptation for developing countries. The first represented a dissemination attempt of the BSCS project, while the second was initiated by the national education authorities, and was carried out by a local curriculum development team.

Curriculum adaptation in developing countries is frequently based on eclectic selection of learning units from a variety of subject-based educational programmes. An example of such an adaptation is the Social Studies programme in Botswana. It organized some elements borrowed from available Social Studies programmes in order to explain to primary and middle school children the inherent values of Botswana's national philosophy known as Kagisano, or social harmony. This philosophy embodies the ideals of democracy, development, self-reliance and unity (Clarken 1990).

While Botswana's Social Studies curriculum represents an exercise in national level adaptation, it nevertheless also implies regional and school based adaptation. As suggested by the National Commission of Education (1977) :

"Unity embraces many important ideas such as loyalty, co-operation and a sense of national identity. It does not mean uniformity, but rather emphasis on common bonds and interests between Botswana's people of different regions, ethnic groups, religions, political parties, or economic circumstances". (p.30).

To live up to this ideal, several elements of the programme have to be adapted at the local level in order to allow an appropriate treatment of values of regional or local significance.

Curriculum integration

Creating links between different bodies of knowledge acquired by schoolgoers has long been a concern of educators. Given the fact that in most schools the curriculum includes various subjects and that during a single day pupils frequently attend lessons in six or seven different subjects, a need has been felt to find ways of reducing the fragmentation of knowledge and conveying a coherent view of man and his environment. The attempt to overcome or reduce the barriers between school subjects and to arrange studies in a way that takes into consideration common elements across different bodies of knowledge is usually referred to as curriculum integration. Some integrative programmes have been prepared by professional teams at curriculum development institutions of various types, but quite frequently integrative topics are developed at the school level, as a school based activity.

Glatthorn and Foshay (1985) provide a historical review and describe various methods of integration, some of which can be observed in schools today. A relatively narrow relation between two or more subjects is represented in the correlated curriculum. Thus, for example, the correlation between physical science and mathematics means that the sequence of topics in physics and mathematics is arranged so that certain advanced techniques in mathematics are taught before problems in physics which can be solved by using these techniques. Cross-disciplinary studies are those in which various disciplines are studied as a single subject. Thus, for example, in the USA 'social studies' appears in the school programme as a single subject combining topics from geography, economics, anthropology, sociology, psychology and sometimes also history. Recently, both at college and high school level, 'area studies' have become popular. These address the problems of a culturally distinct geographic area by the use of a comprehensive range of disciplines, including history, literature, geography and local languages. Examples are Hispanic studies, South East Asian studies and African studies. Another cross-disciplinary study is found in general science or integrated science, in which disciplines like biology, physics, chemistry, geology and astronomy are combined into one subject. In the 1980s, *Science, Technology and Society* (STS) emerged as a widely taught school subject. Solomon (1989) described this subject as "essentially interdisciplinary in that it aims to explore the interactions between science knowledge, technological application, and the social context which direct the endeavours and either benefits or suffers from the results" (p.668). Programme units are mostly problem-based, which enables each community to base studies on its particular problems. Among the topics dealt within these units are issues of national or local importance, like mineral wealth, health, and nutrition.

In developing countries integrated curricula have been initiated and supported by the central educational authorities or development agencies, but there are cases of grass-root initiative, too. Several integrated programmes focused on regional or rural development issues and had a strong practical bias. Fitzgerald (1990) described a large-scale environmental education programme that began in 1985 in the Welo region of Ethiopia. The aims of the programme were formulated jointly by the Ministry of Education and the Swedish International Development Authority (SIDA). The programme focused on halting environmental degradation, and in dealing with this issue it tried to pull together knowledge and ideas from various sources and areas of life.

In 1989, in the regional capital Dese, approximately 3,500 educational personnel received training focusing on the integrated programme and issues of programme implementation. The specific topics to be dealt with were: developing terraces, constructing check-dams, planting trees, carrying out experiments in agro-forestry. Due to its practical bias the programme paid little attention to principles and generalizations underlying the recommended routes of actions. Fitzgerald (1990) pointed out the difficulties in establishing an adequate balance between the practical and the theoretical components of a programme of this type, and claimed that emphasizing relevance might negatively affect the pursuit of academic rigour.

Supplementary curriculum materials

Curriculum materials which do not constitute a part of the regular curriculum are referred to as supplementary curriculum materials. By regular curriculum are meant those items that teachers are required to use in their routine work. These usually are furnished as a curriculum kit containing a set of items such as a syllabus, textbook, published workbooks, resource units, a teacher's handbook and source book, and evaluation instruments. The items may also be bought separately, and in some schools or school systems teachers may be required to produce some of these items. The supplementary curriculum materials consist worksheets, revision exercises, newspaper and periodical clippings, audio or video recordings, film loops or short films, pictures, models, charts, games and computer discs. These serve to facilitate the mastery of those curricular objectives which are contained in the regular curriculum. At the school level teachers may select supplementary materials from those available at the market or may develop such materials as a co-operative endeavour with their peers or by themselves.

Curriculum experts differentiate between supplementary materials, aimed to increase the effectiveness of the teaching of an agreed upon curriculum, and enrichment materials, which broaden its scope (Thomas 1985a, 1985b). In practice, however, it may be difficult to distinguish between the two. Nevertheless, following the common terminology, the topic of curriculum enrichment will be dealt with separately.

As specified above, the items contained in the list of regular curriculum materials differ from those listed as supplementary materials. Nevertheless, specifying the characteristics of a particular curriculum item do not necessarily reveal whether it is a part of the regular curriculum or the supplementary materials. Thus, for example, demonstration materials or games may be contained in the regular curriculum kit, although they are most frequently a product of the teacher's initiative.

Thomas (1985a) distinguishes between three types of supplementary materials: (a) plans for activities, (b) topical or illustrative material supportive of subject matter, (c) verbal and pictorial products and equipment.

(a) Activities refer to *activities* other than reading or speaking about something. Such activities may increase learning efficiency. They increase students' motivation and lead to better understanding.

(b) The second category is subject-matter-related *material*. This may present to the learner recent information on issues related to the topics of their study. Thus, for example, a newspaper review of the performance in the local theatre of a play taught in the school, articles published on the occasion of the anniversary of a national or international historical event, a TV programme about a particular country transmitted on the occasion of a visit of a sports team or important political personality from that country, can be used in the class in the context of teaching a particular topic, not only to motivate students, but also to establish links between what is taught in the school and what captures public interest outside it. An example of supplementary materials of this type is the commemoration of the two hundredth anniversary of the French Revolution in 1989 across the whole world. In most countries articles of various types were published about the far reaching consequences of this event, and one may assume that a great many teachers used such materials as supplementary resources while teaching this topic in their classes.

(c) The third category of supplementary materials consists of *verbal* and *pictorial* products and equipment of various types. This category contains also catalogues and guide books of resources which can be used by teachers and students. A list of libraries and resource centres, annotated bibliographies about relevant books, catalogues of available audiovisual articles, together with guidelines for obtaining them, are of great importance for teaching effectively. Manuals for operating instruments constitute another group of items in this category. Numerous reports, catalogues and guides prepared by public and commercial bodies provide useful orientation for teachers and pupils.

Teachers should bear in mind the need to check the accuracy of the information contained in such materials. They have to ascertain their relevance to particular needs or local circumstances, and encourage pupils to use these resources by demonstration of their worth. Quite frequently, local conditions do not permit the use of publicly available guides and catalogues, and suitable materials of this type need to be prepared locally. Teachers have to assume a leading role in carrying out work of this type. It is their responsibility to ensure that such materials should suit the reading level of their pupils and that the notes describing the characteristic features of each item should represent relevant experiences accumulated in the local context.

Enrichment materials

Enrichment materials serve to expand the objectives of the regular curriculum. They provide an opportunity for students to acquire knowledge, to internalize values and to master skills which are related to the curricular topics dealt with in a course of studies, but exceed the breadth and the depth of coverage of the regular curriculum. Enrichment materials become necessary in the following cases:

1. A particular class has above-average ability and may reach a higher level of achievement than the standard of the curriculum. In certain countries, schools may offer advanced courses for students of high ability bestowing academic credits acknowledged by institutions of higher education.
2. The teacher has a special interest in further elaborating a particular topic, or local circumstances justify or encourage this.
3. Recent events or developments in politics, economics, science, or technology may change the focus of interest in a particular subject and must be taken into account in the school programme.
4. A school may concentrate on or excel in certain studies or activities (such as art, physical education, or mathematics) and it may pursue a policy of admitting students who are interested in extended studies of the type offered by the school. In Hungary, for example, selected schools and classes schedule 10-12 weekly

periods of mathematics in the secondary school timetable, and other schools follow this pattern in other subject areas.

These cases represent two types of reasons for broadening the scope of studies in a subject: Firstly, the predilection of persons involved in making decisions about the curriculum and secondly significant events outside the school related to what is being taught in the school.

Thomas (1985b) distinguishes between two types of curriculum enrichment materials: extension of the regular programme and individualized enrichment.

He also suggests two criteria for evaluating curriculum extension. These are educational importance (curriculum planners may be asked to answer the question whether the enrichment materials will profit the learners or the community) and replacement importance (since adding new topics to the existing curriculum requires time, it may be necessary to reduce time allocated to other topics in the same subject or other subjects, in which case one has to answer the question why the enrichment topic is more important than the topics it replaces). The second type of enrichment is the individualized one. Such materials are intended not for the whole class but only for selected individuals in the class. These may be talented students or those who reveal a special interest in a subject related topic or skill.

Individualized enrichment materials may vary in the length of time they require. One can devise short 2-3 minute assignments or longer ones. Examples of individual assignments of varying extent are listed by Thomas (1985b:1184):

"Examples of experiences requiring only a few minutes are : assign a pupil to read a single passage in a story and answer one question about the passage, or to create three questions to test classmates' understanding of the science topic just studied, or to draw a pencil sketch of the imagined appearance of the hero from a story the class has been reading. Examples of longer term activities are: assign a student to construct a model of a village from an historical event just studied, or to read the biographies of famous scientists, or to write descriptions of a historical incident on the basis of interviews the student has carried out with three elderly members of the community".

Thomas (1985b:1185) suggests three criteria for judging the suitability of individualized enrichment materials:

"(a) Worthwhile objectives -- did the activity teach the student something of real value or merely provide trivial information or worthless skills? (b) New knowledge and heightened skills -- did the activity enable the student to learn something new and achieve higher levels of skills, or did it merely repeat something the student had already mastered? (c) Classroom-management efficiency -- did the activity require an undue amount of teacher time, so that the learning of the rest of the class members suffered? Did the activity distract other students from their studies?".

1. Remedial or corrective learning materials

A unique type of supplementary learning material comes to serve the needs of slow learners or of those who have difficulties in mastering a particular element of the curriculum. For many highly structured school curricula such remedial and corrective materials are produced by the development team and are contained in the regular curriculum kit, but mostly it is the responsibility of the teacher or of a group of teachers to prepare them. To some degree, remedial and corrective curriculum activities constitute a part of the regular curriculum. Good teachers have always paid attention to the needs of those who have not mastered the course materials, but in overcrowded classes slower learners might be ignored. Lundgren (1972) finds that teachers have different expectations of what proportion of their students should master the taught material. Some are satisfied with 50 per cent while more exacting teachers would start to teaching a new topic only when approximately 70 per cent of the class has mastered the previous topic taught. Generally, in the regular instructional framework too demanding an approach may unacceptably slow down the pacing of the curriculum for the class, and average and above average students will learn much less than they are capable of.

The mastery learning strategy emphasizes the importance of systematically testing the achievement level of students and making decisions about what to teach in the class, for the whole group and for each individual, on the basis of his or her actually measured levels of achievement.

The mastery learning strategy uses pre-planned remedial or corrective learning materials. Teaching is done after assessing students knowledge of a new topic in relation to an expected level of knowledge. After a particular unit of the curriculum is taught, those who pass a criterion-referenced mastery test of all the objectives of the curriculum unit may move on to the next unit. At this point teachers are expected to provide individually tailored corrective learning materials to the students who failed the mastery test. Teachers are expected to prepare remedial materials for each of the objectives contained in the curricular materials. The individualized corrective materials are administered either in extra study time or during scheduled study time, when students with an advanced level of knowledge provide peer tutoring to those who need help.

The mastery learning strategy is based on the well-documented assumption that with high-quality teaching approximately 90 per cent of the learners can be expected to master the curricular objectives.

In general, the remedial or corrective curriculum materials may be of the following types:

1. Additional exercises of the type administered in class (the number of exercises done in class may be insufficient for some learners to reach a level of mastery in a particular topic).

2. Prerequisite knowledge: the preparation of mastery learning curriculum units depends on establishing the prerequisite knowledge and corrective materials for those who have not attained it.

3. Analysis of a complex problem into its basic components, and exercises for dealing with these components separately before combining them into the complex single problem.

4. Providing additional or alternative cues for students on how to deal with a particular problem.

The mastery learning strategy has been used intensively in several developing countries. Its contribution in raising the achievement level of learners was acknowledged in a recent panel meeting at the *Asian Centre of Educational Innovation for Development* (ACEID) by the participants representing nineteen Asian and Pacific region states (ACEID 1990). Through collective deliberation the panel identified ten mega-trends in the curriculum reforms observed in developing countries. These basic trends, in their view, have specific implications for the content of the school curriculum in all subjects, and at both the primary and secondary levels. One of these mega-trends is the utilization of the mastery learning strategy.

Studies about the effectiveness of mastery learning were carried out in various developing countries. In Malaysia, Nordin (1980) examined the relative importance of various components of the mastery learning strategy (such as cues and participation), and found its strongest component to be the utilization of feedback and correctives. Kim's (1975) study in South Korea is probably the largest experimental design type study which has ever been carried out for examining the effectiveness of a teaching strategy. The original mastery learning strategy was adjusted to the special circumstances of South Korea, where classes include 70 pupils, consequently making it impossible to apply an individualized approach to teaching. The findings of this large scale experimental study proved the effectiveness of the treatment.

Another example of using corrective materials developed at school level is provided by Okpala and Onocha (1988). Without directly referring to mastery learning method, they tried to identify difficult learning topics in advanced high school physics courses in Nigeria. On basis of the O-level physics syllabus, they compiled a list of 53 topics and asked students to indicate the extent of difficulties they encountered in learning each one of them. This needs-assessment type study may provide orientation to teachers about the nature of supplementary study materials required for a particular group of students, and thus motivate teachers initiating SBCD activities.

While in the above mentioned cases the remedial or corrective teaching materials were produced by the monitoring agencies, in most cases additional corrective exercises were produced at the school level. Thus, use of the mastery learning strategy challenges teachers to produce instructional materials to suit any particular target population.

2. *Topics of local interest*

Topics of local interest may be dealt with in the framework of a particular subject or in an integrated course of several cognate disciplines.

The most frequently used local interest topics are included in geography studies. Indeed, the first curricular units in geography deal with phenomena related to the childs close environment. The first steps in learning to use the geographical map are structured according to the 'proximal-distal' principle, starting with topics related to the child's close vicinity, thus enabling integration of the child's personal experiences with formal studies in the school. Such curriculum units can be best prepared at local level with the active participation of local teachers. Most school subjects contain topics of local interest, like local history or history of famous personalities with local connections; multi-cultural studies focusing on the culture of various groups in the local community, art treasures available in local museums, the local trade and industry and career opportunities, the economic resources of the location, the flora and fauna of a given region -- all these topics need to be dealt with in the school programme and the preparation of curriculum materials covering topics of this type can be done at local level.

An example of producing a small oral history project as a co-operative venture in four rural primary schools is described by Evans (1989). Primary school children carried out tape recorded interviews with senior citizens of the community. The information collected in this way was transcribed and distributed to all children participating in the project. Small teams were organized and each team focused on summarizing a particular aspect of the history of the place. The recordings collected by the children and their summaries were deposited in local archives and they may serve as resource material for future age-cohorts in the schools.

Another example of local history study is described by Graham (1988). His project was conducted in a mixed ability secondary school in the United Kingdom. It was carried out as a collaborative project of the history and geography department with occasional help from crafts and English teachers, and the support of the Local History Society. The study focused on a particular period of time. The students used primary and secondary sources. A bibliography of printed publications relevant to the topic was compiled; documents, pictures, photos and census data available in the archives were examined; historical remnants of the period were studied. The teacher responsible for the project prepared a guideline for carrying out local history studies. He also referred to the 'spin-off' of such a project:

"... it is a great aid in obtaining the active support of your colleagues to outline the 'spin-offs' and personal advancement that may materialise from the work. These include, and I make no apologies for the mercenary tone, such motives as:

- enhancement of credibility with pupils as it displays teacher effort in an area with universal appeal to all age groups, i.e. necessitates co-operation and the teacher and pupils having to learn together;

- increased promotion prospects both within and outside the school;

- enhances the reputation of the school with parents and other interested parties;

- gives personal status within the community as a teacher interested in your area". [Graham 1988, p. 27]

An example of adding supplementary units dealing with issues of local significance to a programme developed by a professional team is provided by the social studies curriculum in the English-speaking Caribbean. Traditionally, the role of social studies in this part of the world has been cast in the mould of knowledge of the past fused with some knowledge of local institutions. Emphasis has been on knowledge and the learning of current information on political, social and economic information.

A joint team of the University of West Indies campuses from Jamaica, Trinidad and Barbados introduced some of the recent trends and current theories into the field of social studies education, and developed a social studies education programme which focuses on training students to become thinking citizens, equipped for, and willing to participate in, the task of nation building.

As indicated by Griffith (1990), any topic in this well-structured social studies programme lends itself to generating topics of local concern which are closely associated with the students' immediate experience. Such units are, of course, best produced by local teams.

3. *Current events*

Current events may instigate schools to quickly develop new instructional modules or to carry out learning activities dealing with the significance of such events. At the system level such work of curriculum development may take a long time, preventing immediate reaction. A delayed treatment of such events may be inappropriate.

One event which certainly motivated many teachers of literature to introduce changes in their course and probably also to produce a new instructional module, was the awarding of the Nobel prize to the Mexican writer Octavio Paz in 1990. An example of dealing in the school with an industrial disaster extensively covered in the mass media is provided by Plant (1988). On April 26, 1986 the nuclear reactor of Chernobyl, Ukraine, USSR, suffered a major explosion. Within a few days a huge cloud of radioactivity was distributed over a large area of North Europe at a distance more than 3000 km. away from the place of the explosion. Due to a heavy rainfall on 2 and 3 May there was a wet deposition of radioactive fall-out on the vegetation in the Upland areas of Britain. In a small seaside town at the seashore on the North Coast the physics teacher, together with his students, carried out a background measure using equipment available at the physics laboratory of the school (a Mullarrd ZP 1481 Geiger-Muller tube in conjunction with a Panax scaler).

Subsequently, for several days count measures were taken using a piece of card approximately 100 mm square. It was found that on 2 and 3 May the count rates were significantly above the background. The cards used on these two days were measured subsequently in order to obtain decay curves for the deposited material. The number of counts per hour in excess of the background was not significant from 8 May onwards. Trying to identify the material and the radiation dosage the experiment led to the conclusion, that the hazard to the public from direct radiation from active material, which has been deposited on the ground, is small, and not more than that one receives on a return flight from London to Paris.

4. New instructional units

SBCD may focus on developing new instructional units. Topics of local interest or those dealing with current events may fall into this category. Additionally schools may develop courses about emerging topics or disciplinary areas which previously were not taught in schools, and therefore no syllabuses or instructional materials have been produced for their study.

An example of a grassroots initiative course in an emerging study area is presented by the Secondary Science Curriculum Review (1987). It consists of a module in biotechnology. A team produced guidelines for teachers, instructional materials for pupils, supplementary worksheets and a set of 36 slides. The team described the course as follows:

"The material explores the historical, social and industrial contexts of science and helps students recognise that the solutions scientists generate to problems may be problematic in themselves. It also encourages the development of 'economic awareness'.

The materials focus on Dairy Biotechnology (yoghurt manufacture), Yeast Technology Today, Washday Biotechnology, Cloning, Genetic Engineering, including a theatre play based on the insulin story. Active learning methods include role-play, experimental problem-solving, data handling, cost analysis, modelling, drama, a

simulated radio broadcast based on the controversial issue
of genetic engineering, and directed activities related to
texts". (p.B01).

Implications

1. Schools should take advantage of the freedom bestowed upon
them to share responsibility with the central authorities in making
decisions about their educational programmes.
2. At the school level, curriculum-related decisions are made by
the principal, the subject-matter co-ordinator, the classroom
teacher, the whole staff, the parents, etc. Schools should strive to
create a consensus about the distribution of decision-making
power among these factors, and should prepare a written
document specifying relevant rules.
3. Schools are advised to distribute decision-making power
about curricular matters among the central management of the
institute, the subject departments and the individual teachers.
4. Decisions about adopting a curriculum and selecting
instructional materials should be made after carefully examining a
broad variety of available alternatives.
5. Agreement should be reached at the school level among all
interested parties about criteria of evaluating curricula and
instructional materials of other types.
6. It is advisable to adopt a curriculum evaluation form, and if
necessary to adapt it to local needs and conditions. Schools may
also produce an evaluation form by borrowing items from a
variety of available forms, or construct their own.
7. School level decisions about adapting available curricula
should be based on serious deliberations in which all interested
parties are given the opportunity to express their opinions.
8. Teachers within a single department or, across departments,
should be encouraged to create links between different bodies of
knowledge. This can be done in the form of establishing
correlation among them or developing integrated curricular units.
It is recommended that at each grade level at least one integrated
topic should be included in the curriculum.

9. Issues and problems of local concern, like environment protection, utilization of local resources, augmenting local job opportunities, may serve as a basis for school-based development of integrated curriculum units.

10. Supplementary materials like enrichment units, remedial materials and independent modules dealing with topics of local interest or current events can be prepared by individual teachers, ad hoc teams from the school, teams from the staff members of several schools or co-operatively by members of the school staff and out-of-school volunteers and experts.

IV. Groups affecting school-based curriculum development

As already indicated, SBCD is a generic term. It describes a variety of curriculum development activities differing from each other from the points of view of scope, purpose, and persons or groups participating in it. At the same time it is also a misleading term because it refers to activities initiated by persons or groups outside the school or in which individual teachers, rather than the school community, revealed interest.

The school's educational programme is affected by statutory regulations which formally determine the rights and obligations of various parties concerned with the school. The national authorities, the regional and district offices, the local educational authorities, and frequently also the parents, are formally granted some rights of intervention. There are also non-statutory groups which exert pressure on the school in matters of determining the curriculum.

Figure 4.1 contains a schematic representation of forces affecting the school's programme. The major factors exerting influence on curriculum decision are the national framework (which in some large or multi-cultural/multi-ethnic countries can be substituted by separate frameworks for the regional, cultural or linguistic sub-systems), the school community (comprising of the teaching and non-teaching staff, the principal and groups directly linked to the school and participating personally in the affairs of the school), and the individual teacher.

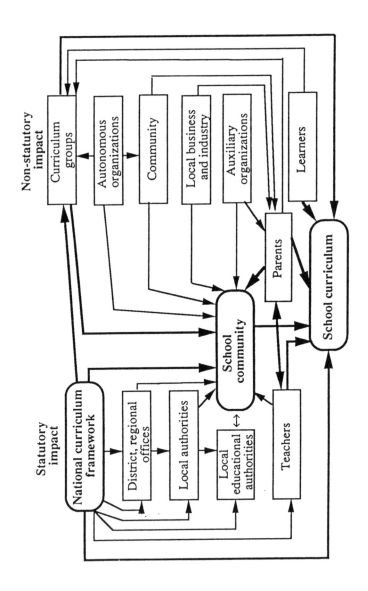

Figure 4.1 Factors affecting school-based curriculum

This section examines the nature of impact of various groups referred to in *Figure 4.1*. Our focus is the SBCD, and therefore most arrows are pointing to the school community and the individual teacher. Factors affecting the national curriculum framework are outside the domain of our interest. The scheme represents the view that the national curriculum framework, the demands of the local educational authorities, and the pressure of non-profit or commercial curriculum groups, all have an important say what happens in schools in terms of SBCD. At the same time the development activities of the curriculum groups are affected primarily by the national framework and secondarily by the demands of the learners and parents.

The statutory impact line

SBCD may be affected by legislation or by other statutory decrees either positively or negatively. The central authorities may move towards devolution of curriculum decision making or may reduce to a minimum the power of other factors in such decisions. In the former case the regional authorities may share power with the central authorities, or may fully substitute them. Furthermore the local authorities and the schools may be given autonomy to decide what to teach.

1. *Local authorities*

The word 'local' in this context refers to situations, where the decisions are made outside the school, while the decision-makers deal with the programme of schools personally known to them and problems and needs they are familiar with. In this respect they differ from central authorities that deal with the curriculum of a large number of schools without having direct and personal contact with those affected by their decisions.

Curriculum decisions at local level deal, usually, with organizational and management aspects of the school programme, or with macro-aspects of the curriculum content. To the first category pertain issues such as streaming or de-streaming and the support for open education patterns. To the second category pertain issues such as the standards of achievement at various grade levels, comprehensive versus multi-cultural-track framework, censorship of books used in the school, the place of sex education in the school programme, and multi-cultural-cultural education. Such decisions also involve selecting subjects to be taught in a particular school from a broad variety of centrally approved subjects or disciplines. This would, for example, include whether to teach typing or technical drawing in a particular school, or which foreign language or art subject should be included in the school's programme.

2. *Educational authorities at the local level*

The local level educational authorities differ across countries in their organizational structure and their involvement in curriculum decisions. In some countries, like England and Wales, the *Local Educational Authorities* (LEAs) are a branch of the local authorities. In other countries, like the USA, each School District has its own School Board, which acts as an independent agency, raises levies, and is not subject to the administrative control of the local authorities. The local educational authorities are likely to initiate curriculum development activities only if demand is imposed upon them to do so. Demand may come from above, that is, from the national government and local authorities, or from below, from the voting constituency. Shipman (1985) claimed that the Local Educational Authorities (LEAs) in England and Wales empowered the school to make decisions about their curriculum and did not initiate curriculum development activities until pressure was applied both from above, from the central government, national committees, and through research reports, as well as from below, from teachers and interest groups. Demands for the School Board involvement in curriculum development are also heard in the USA. A national survey conducted in the USA revealed that most school districts prefer a 'home-grown' curriculum, and more than two thirds of the districts have a master plan for curriculum development (Martin et al. 1987).

Involvement in the curriculum of authorities at the local-level is felt not only in organising curriculum development teams or producing curriculum materials. But also in the great variety of initiatives which do not directly involve the curriculum but which, nevertheless, have an impact on what is taught in schools. The maintenance of resource centres, the organization of in-service courses, the administration of achievement surveys, and information gathering questionnaires sent to schools serve multiple purposes, and among others they inform schools about what they are expected to teach.

3. *The school community*

Modern theories of educational organization describe schools as a loosely coupled system, characterized by the following traits (Ecker 1985):

a. Unclear goals: Even if schools define their goals in terms like 'excellence' or 'quality of instruction', they encounter difficulties in operationally defining these terms.
b. Unclear technology: The transmission of knowledge is little understood and little rationalized.
c. Fluid participation: The participation of staff members in different activities is not stable.

Nevertheless, curriculum development is based on team work, and it can be effectively done only if the legitimacy of such an activity is fully supported by a cohesive group within the institute. Wolfe et al. (1989) argues that the school community consists of four groups: the principal and other senior administrative task holders, the teachers, the parents and the learners. They view the interrelationships among these four groups as an important factor in determining the success of any school-based initiative. The community spirit of the school is enhanced by norms, values and beliefs that include collaboration, collegiality, cohesiveness, support, commitment, open communication, shared decision making, co-operation, ownership and belonging.

The roles of the administration, including the principal, and the teachers will now be taken up, while the involvement of the parents and the learners will be examined in the following section dealing with the non-statutory impacts.

(i) The principal

It is the role of the principal to energize the school community. Wolfe et al. (1989) suggest a series of activities which may create a sense of community, like establishing a school governor's team, introducing team teaching and co-operative learning. Summarizing studies which deal with the school community, they provide the following list of behaviours which should characterize the behaviour of the principal:

- Promotes open communication and shared decision-making between teachers, students, parents and administrators.
- Provides opportunities for enhancing collegial relations.
- Seeks agreement about the mission of the school.
- Promotes a strong school spirit.

In Sri Lanka, in the context of the development and implementation of an innovative rural education programme, one of the important phases of the planning was running a workshop for principals of rural primary schools. The workshop was designed to bring new dimensions to the roles of the principals. Previously, the stress in management was on administration leaving a vacuum in the academic and pedagogic aspects of school life. The objectives of the workshop were, among others, to develop (a) the ability and the knowledge of methodology for identifying community resources, (b) the ability to integrate teaching/learning in the world of work and the cultural milieu of the community, (c) positive attitudes towards the dignity of labour, (d) awareness about the potential of rural learning resources for teaching/learning (Ekanayake 1990).

A comprehensive treatment of the principals role in SBCD is presented by Schwab (1983). He argues for the principal's participation in SBCD activities, but emphasizes that the principal should not serve as the chairman of the committee dealing with such matters. Participation is important, because the principal's knowledge and approval of a new programme is critical for the effective installation of the change. Secondly, the principal, if long enough in that position, may have the fullest knowledge of those factors which affect teaching and learning in the school. On the other hand, serving as a chairman entails the danger that the chairman of the group would act as an administrator rather than as an 'educational expert'. According to Schwab, the co-ordinator of the curriculum group should be seen by the teachers as one of theirs and not as a superior authority.

(ii) The teachers

The curriculum reform of the 1960s viewed the process of curriculum development as a highly professional activity to be carried out by specially trained experts, and in which teachers may fulfil only marginal roles. Teachers were invited to participate in the work of the professional development teams, but mostly only in a part-time capacity or as being seconded from their regular jobs for a limited period of time. The classroom experience of the teacher was considered to be a useful and important source of professional knowledge needed for making curriculum decisions of some types, but it was judged to be less than sufficient for carrying out the work of curriculum developers. Experts working at curriculum development centers revealed more sensitivity to the teachers' lack of ability to use their sophisticated curriculum rather than to their own lack of experience dealing with classroom situations. Aware of the fact that the teacher is a necessary mediator between the centrally produced curriculum and its target population, curriculum experts designed curriculum guides that specified the teacher's action in detail, and organised intensive in-service courses to ensure that teachers would do in the class what the curriculum planners believed they should do. Connelly and Clandinin (1988: p. 138) described this attitude by saying: "Teachers were seen as modifying screens of the purposes built into the materials." Therefore, various strategies were undertaken to minimize teacher influence, and materials of this type were considered to be 'teacher-proof' materials.

In the 1970s it became apparent that these centrally developed, highly sophisticated programmes did not succeed in changing teaching practice. Teachers frequently did not understand the new materials, did not identify with the innovation and continued to teach as they did before. The belief in the possibility of producing teacher-proof materials was shaken and the reputation of the teacher as being competent to deal with curricular matters was restored. Teachers were asked to increase their involvement in producing curricula, and their participation in this process has now been accepted as a necessary feature of development.

By 1990 the view which favours a teacher-proof curriculum had been fully repudiated. Educators recognized that it was virtually impossible to prepare curriculum materials on which teachers could not imprint their personal stamp. The strong belief in the desirability of the teacher's involvement in curriculum development, and in his or her competency to do such work was reflected in the term curriculum-proof teacher which came to ridicule the ill-conceived idea of teacher-proof curricula.

Teachers' involvement in curriculum development can be observed in developing countries, too, but with lower frequency than in developed countries. In developing countries, teachers' involvement in SBCD is greatly dependent on obtaining support from external agencies. Sutaria (1990) described a large-scale project in the Philippines known as the *Program for Decentralized Educational Development* (PRODED). Its goal was 'teaching for maximum learning'. The programme was launched in 1983 in response to the results of the national Survey of Outcomes of Elementary Education, which revealed that pupils mastered less than half of the competencies expected for their grade levels. The central educational authorities defined a list of minimum competencies for each grade level and set an operational objective for all schools to raise the number of goals attained by the pupils each year by two per cent. Teachers were encouraged to develop supplementary materials suitable for the unique needs. The author noted that:

> "schools that had an abundance of locally developed materials designed for learners of various abilities registered better performance than those that had a little number. The self-instructional modules were particularly useful in getting people more involved in their own learning" (p. 248).

A cautionary note against exaggerated hopes with regard to the teachers' involvement in curriculum development is well articulated by Hargreaves (1989). He claims that teachers are present-oriented, conservative, individualistic, try to avoid long-term planning, have difficulties in incorporating in their daily work continuous collaboration with others and often resist involvement in whole school decision-making.

But despite the doubts expressed by Hargreaves, the most active partners in curriculum development activities are the teachers. The scope of their activity may be limited, but it constitutes a significant contribution to enhancing the identity of the school and its community spirit.

The non-statutory impact line

Some factors have an impact on SBCD even without there being formal empowerment for their intervention in the school's programme. Paradoxically enough large-scale centralistic curriculum projects, such as the American *Biological Science Curriculum Study*, where adopted, generated intensive SBCD activities. Teachers, impressed by the quality of the programme, tried to adapt it to local conditions, to develop supplementary modules of local interest, and even to develop new programme modules, imitating the features of such 'imported curricula'.

This section deals with the impact of the community, including voluntary and auxiliary organizations, and business and industrial bodies operating inside the community. It also deals with the involvement of parents and learners in deciding what should be taught in schools. In some educational systems parents and learners right of involvement has some statutory basis, but since in most countries this right is not clearly stated, let alone operationalized and realized, it seems appropriate to deal with them in this section.

(iv) The community

There is a growing trend of forging strong relationships between schools and the communities served by them. Schools are expected to respond to local needs both through what is taught in the classes and through providing facilities for programmes serving the community's adult population. At the same time the community is expected to recruit resources for the school and to co-operate with it in ensuring that the curriculum satisfies local needs.

Ideal as this relationship seems to be, the involvement of community groups in the professional aspects of school life is not always welcomed by the teachers. Teachers' Unions, too, frequently view this mutual dependency as an infringement upon the professional autonomy of the teacher. Nevertheless, the benefits of co-operative action between schools and communities outweigh its drawbacks.

The community's right of involvement is rooted in the democratic principle that public services should operate in a way which satisfies the expectations of their sponsor. The necessity of the latters involvement is rooted in the fact that teachers may come to work from a distant geographic area, and their cultural, social and linguistic background may be different from that of the school's population, so that without close co-operation with the community's adult population they would encounter difficulties in responding to local needs.

The community's curriculum-related orientation can be conveyed to schools through various channels. Informal statements made at occasional gatherings, celebrations or public events by influential persons may contain messages which should be considered by the school in making curricular decisions. But the direct involvement of organized bodies within the community, or representing the community, is a more powerful way of exerting pressure on the school. In some educational systems communities are legally empowered to organize advisory committees with full or limited authority to make curriculum related decisions. Churches, religious institutions, commercial, industrial and agricultural bodies representing the need of certain sub-groups of the community, local organizations, or local branches of national voluntary organizations all may exert pressure to include some topics in the school programme. Some national voluntary organizations have established liaison offices for dealing with schools. In many cases they also produce curriculum materials, and they are interested in using their local branches to disseminate these materials in the local schools. Voluntary organizations all over the world deal with issues of environmental protection, preservation of wildlife, health care, preservation of historical monuments, cultivation of local traditions, home industries, science clubs, creative arts, etc.

Also, auxiliary organizations which were established to assist the school in specific matters, or to represent the interest of minority groups or special interest groups among the student population, may have an impact on school-based curriculum decisions.

The reaction of the school to the needs of the community may be responsive or initiatory. It may concede to community demands, or it may initiate contact with agencies operating in the community to help the school adjust its programme to local needs.

In developing countries, strong links between schools and communities served by them have been observed in most countries concerned with rural development. Ekanayake (1990) described a programme of this type in Sri Lanka which aimed at having an impact on rural people and helping them to meet their future needs. As a preparatory activity for producing curriculum units which deal with locally relevant topics, the curriculum planning team visited rural communities and identified sites, situations, personnel, etc. which may serve as Rural Educational Resources (RER), and constitute a target of curriculum units. They listed twenty-three such items including (a) human resources (like the village physician, eye specialist, funeral officer), (b) craft and commercial resources (like the blacksmith, pottery, tile-making industry, stores, garage), (c) institutions (like the religious center, agricultural productivity center, hand-loom center) and (d) natural resources (like a small tributary of a river). School-based teams aided by experts were invited to develop learning experiences utilizing these resources for various grade levels of the primary school. These locally relevant topics were expected to assist in the socialization of the pupils for the cultural, social and economic environment of their village. Links between the school and the community were strengthened through the following activities:

1. Organizing community awareness programmes through school development societies and village level officials in order to create awareness of the aims and purposes of the new design.
2. Organizing committees in the village. The function of the committees could be : (a) developing study sites; (b) organizing study centers; (c) sharing responsibility with those who volunteer; (d) evaluating and monitoring progress.
3. Organizing exhibitions in the school and developing local museums which may contain local artefacts, contrivances, products, stories/books written about the village life.

4. Parents' involvement

Parents constitute a special sub-group of the community characterized by being obliged to maintain some contact with the school. According to Berger (1987), parents are very interested in all aspects of their children's education. They differ from school administrators and teachers in their desire for more involvement in decision-making. School staff want more involvement of parents in supporting the school programme but little parental involvement in decision-making about the life in the school.

Berger distinguishes between six school related parental educational activities:
1. Parents help children to learn, supervise their homework.
2. They are spectators in the school, attend school performances in which their children are involved.
3. They are accessory volunteers, rendering non-educational services to school, such as raising funds, maintaining the building and equipment.
4. They provide para-professional educational services, in the capacity of teacher aid, etc.
5. As resource persons they may help the teacher by coming to the class and providing supplementary information derived from their personal or professional experience about curriculum related topics. Moreover they may motivate the teacher to teach topics which are related to the parents personal expertise.
6. As policy makers they may be involved in the process of decision-making about various issues related to the school.

Only the two last activities touch upon curriculum related issues, and one of them, the parents' role as resource person, plays a marginal role in curricular decisions.

Public opinion surveys in the USA indicate that the school's curriculum is one of the three major school related concerns of the parent (the other two being discipline and drug abuse). Nevertheless, in numerous educational systems across the world, parental right to participate in decisions about the curriculum is not anchored in the law. Thus, in Australia, where the central educational authorities monitored a gradual devolution of decision-making power, or in England and Wales, where a new nationally prescribed curriculum framework was introduced, the responsibility for curriculum was delegated to the regional and local authorities, while the right of the parents has not been clearly defined. In the USA, too, the school site advisory council may or may not have members whose children study in the schools of their responsibility. Parents may ask the help of the court if they are not satisfied with the school's operation but they do not have direct access to the process of decision-making. On the other hand, there are educational systems such as Indonesia and Hungary where, by law, parents have the right to determine the content of a given percentage (usually 20-30 per cent) of the whole school programme. However, none of these arrangements guarantees smooth co-operation between schools and parents. Co-operation requires initiative and leadership. While both parties may initiate co-operative action, schools are usually more adept at initiating and providing leadership than are parents. Indeed parents frequently do not constitute a homogeneous group, and it may well happen that the interest of one group of parents contradicts the interest of another. In such cases the school leadership has to initiate action and work out a solution acceptable to all conflicting parties.

The school's capability to identify areas of consensus in which teachers, parents and pupils can co-operate may create a favourable climate in the school which, in turn, may lead to a partnership with parents in making decisions about various curriculum-related issues. An example of such triple co-operation in developing a health based physical education programme is described by Hulbert (1987). The programme developers created a questionnaire about health related views, opinions and behaviours and asked the children to answer the questions together with their parents at their homes. Illustrative items from the questionnaires are presented in *Table 4.1*.

Table 4.1   Questions answered jointly by children and their parents

	%
Taking part in physical activities can improve a person's fitness	3.2
Jogging can strengthen a person's heart	52
A lot of backaches are caused because people don't have strong enough muscles in their stomachs	70.8
Taking part in vigorous exercise releases chemicals into the blood which can make you feel "high"	4.15
Sugar is an unnecessary part of our diet	48.8
For some people too much salt in their diet can increase the risk of suffering from a stroke or heart disease	13.8

Percentage of sample who gave incorrect response or were "not sure" about the truth of the statements

Source: Hulbert, L. (1987). *Health based physical education: the need to involve parents,* Bulletin of Physical Education, p.11.

The summary of the questions served as a basis for planning jointly with the parents a physical education programme for the children.

An example from Malaysia about co-operation between parents and teachers to increase the relevance of the curriculum for solving daily life problems is described by Aziz et al (1990).

"An initial activity of the project was an attempt to raise parents' awareness of their roles in education through dialogues and discussions with the headman and members of the community, informal get-together and demonstration sessions. Having gained a favourable response, community centers were set up where workshops were organized ....for developing suitable teaching-learning materials for school and home use. Some of these materials include reading passages, picture cards and educational games". (p. 60-61)

It should be noted, however, that parents' co-operation with schools may depend on the existence of an adequate climate, and in many cases there is a need for providing suitable training. Stromquist (1986) described an attempt to decentralize educational decision-making in Peru. It turned out that the innovation suggested by the central educational authorities appealed to neither the teachers nor the parents. Due to the Teachers Union's opposition, the teachers refused to co-operate with the Ministry of Education in implementing the suggested change. Parents received neither training nor encouragement to fulfil such a role. The administrative staff of the Ministry did not know how to implement this change. Finally, the whole idea of decentralization had to be abandoned.

5. *Learner participation in curriculum decisions*

Educators have concerned themselves with learner participation in decisions about the curriculum for two reasons. The first is that if learners have an interest in a topic of studies their motivation to learn is enhanced. The second is that the ideal of self-determination or the democratization of school life is promoted if learners are considered as partners in determining the course of their own studies.

A student-centered approach in making curriculum decisions has been advocated in Sri Lanka and Thailand, hoping to enable students to solve problems, to seek additional knowledge by themselves, and to apply such knowledge to daily life situations (Aziz et al 1990).

Surveys to find out what topics learners were interested in were carried out as a preparatory activity for several large-scale curriculum development projects. Thus, for example, in the US, the *Children Television Workshop* (CTW) used various techniques to discover what kinds of programmes children liked. Children were presented with a large selection of photographs covering a wide range of topics such as animals, spaceships, plants, insects, and requested to rank the pictures in order of interest.

In another technique children were requested to communicate the questions or problems that preoccupied them in order to determine the appeal of various topics. As may be expected, the originality of the questions asked by children exceeded the imagination of adults. Some examples were:
- How does the body know when it is time to grow?
- Why do zebras have stripes?
- How do you make chalk?
- Is there a real Santa Claus?
- Why do I sometimes feel like I have no friends?

There is little consensus among educators on the desirability, let alone the desirable scope, of learners' involvement in curriculum decisions. At one end of the continuum are those who recognize the instrumental value of considering learners' interest. Thus, for example, Smith et al. (1957, p.603) argue that the "interests of the individual learner are not a sufficient criterion of curriculum content, [but] they are necessary criterion". At the other extreme are those who claim that learners should be given full freedom to make decisions about their own programme as long as they remain within the framework prescribed by the school.

Learners' involvement in curriculum development can be described in terms of:

- the nature of the development activity;
- the scope of the curriculum elements over which learners may have a say;
- the locus of the initiative.

Nature of the development activity: Learner involvement in curriculum decisions is usually limited to selecting a course of studies, but there are numerous examples of learners preparing instructional materials. It is almost universally accepted practice to offer electives in secondary schools. Pupils may be allowed to select a particular subject from electives offered by the school. The school often invites pupils to suggest subjects or topics for inclusion in their programme.

Scope of curriculum elements: Learner decisions may relate to macro-elements of study or micro-elements only. Opting for a particular elective may mean a commitment of several years. For example, deciding to study a certain foreign language or art subject may require continuous study for two or three years or even more. Alternatively, the decision may consist in selecting a particular unit in a modularly structured course or a particular assignment in a lesson. Often, sets of instructional materials contain a wide selection of assignments differing in content, level of difficulty, organization (individual or co-operative), nature of mental operation (such as reading and writing, hands-on work, observing phenomena, talking to people, carrying out art work, etc.). Where there is assignment choice one must learn to select, or in other words, to build up a personalized curriculum.

Schools may have various institutional arrangements for fostering a personalized curriculum. Examples are several variations of what is called independent studies. Pupils may study a particular subject, or a topic in it, which is not included in the regular curriculum. In this case use is made of available self-instructional materials. Pupils may carry out small-scale research studies, either individually or on a co-operative basis, under the guidance of a teacher or an outside expert volunteering to serve as a mentor. Sometimes the topic of such independent studies is negotiated with the teacher and the agreement is specified in a curriculum contract.

The locus of the initiative: The initiative for involving students in curriculum related decisions may come from outside the school, like the central educational authorities, the community or the parents. It may instead be school-based or teacher-based. In numerous educational systems the national curriculum prescribes that schools should provide alternatives to select from, or establish some type of partnership with learners in making decisions about the curriculum.

Collaboration

Curriculum development is teamwork which can be carried out by the teachers of a single school or through collaboration between teachers from several schools, or through collaboration between schools and support services from outside the school. During the 1980s schools most commonly developed curricula in partnership with universities, institutes of teacher training and other institutes of higher education.

De Bevoise (1986) mentioned several reasons for the universities willingness to enter into partnership with schools in the field of curriculum development. *Firstly*, universities redefined their roles and ceased to view themselves as institutions responsible only for research and teaching, instead committing themselves to direct social involvement. Universities are now consciously dedicated to serving the surrounding area and thus enhancing linkage with the community. *Secondly*, universities and particularly schools of education, realized that close contact with schools is necessary for generating knowledge which may contribute to the improvement of education. The curriculum of teacher education was broadened to include observing life in the school, carrying out experiments, trailling new teaching methods and instructional materials. Schools could serve as laboratories for generating knowledge about education. All these activities required partnership with the schools. *Thirdly*, universities became aware that improved high school teaching may raise the entry level knowledge of students being admitted to the universities. Thus, involvement in the high school programme provides a service for the university, too. Finally, collaborative studies, if supported by funds from external bodies, agencies or local or national educational authorities, increase the university's resources.

Collaboration in curriculum development between universities and schools may take different forms. One type of collaboration is an agreement between a university and a group of schools, according to which each of the two partners may initiate action, and each project or programme is carried out by an ad hoc team. A group of teachers may invite an expert from the collaborating university to work with them on a particular project, and several curriculum projects, can be carried out simultaneously by groups of small teams. University staff members may be invited to lecture in high school classes, and high school teachers may be invited to speak about their teaching experiences to university students and faculty members. Collaboration of this type enables grassroot initiative on a broad scale.

In most cases the initiative comes from universities. University-based projects recruit teachers or accept those who apply for admission as partners in curriculum development. The partners of such collaborative endeavour respect each others professional expertise and neither of them strives to be dominant in the group.

McGowan and Williams (1990) examined the impact of school-university partnership and found that it may create meaningful changes in the school's curriculum if the partnership is flexible, situation-specific, practitioner-formulated and monitored, interactive, relatively egalitarian, systematic and directed at a problem which participants perceive as relevant.

An example of collaboration of this type is the *Children's Learning in Science Project* (CLISP) of the University of Leeds, United Kingdom.

6. Two instances of collaboration with universities in curriculum development

The curriculum development activities of the *Children's Learning Science Project* (CLISP) in the University of Leeds (United Kingdom) are an example of collaboration between a university and a group of 30 teachers. The teachers, under the guidance of an expert team from the university, developed and trailled teaching schemes in various areas of science teaching.

The purpose of the project is to produce curriculum materials based on the constructivist view of learning. The project selects only commonly taught curriculum contents and develops curriculum materials which follow the pattern of a particular teaching method.

The basis of the constructivist view is that children construct their own knowledge through personal interaction with natural phenomena and social interaction with adults and peers (Needham 1987). Since children already have notions how things happen in the world before they come to study formal science, it is important for the teacher first to find out their ideas about topics being taught and then to let them reflect about these ideas, compare them with those of others, and evaluate the usefulness of these ideas alongside the teacher's scientific theories.

The characteristic features of this project is illustrated here by the outline of a curriculum unit on plant nutrition. (See *Figure 4.2*). The unit consists of three main sections: testing pupils's ideas, exploration of the school-science (or the teacher's) ideas, and application of the school-science idea. The same structure is employed in other units produced by the Centre.

Another instance of collaboration between schools and an institution of higher education occurred in the curriculum development activities of the *Integrated Rural Development* (IRD) project in Bunumbu, Sierra Leone. The entire project was an experiment to confront some of the national and sectional problems faced by the people of the country. One of these problems was the fact that the educational system, normally the supplier of the required manpower, and an influential social agent failed to meet the demands. As noted by Banya (1989) education was bookish and strongly reflected the traditions of the British system. Bunumbu Teachers' College, the single institute of higher education operating in the region, was asked to assume responsibility for monitoring curriculum development for the formal and informal educational frameworks. The college co-operated with 20 schools within a 20 mile radius. They served mainly as pilot schools for trying out new learning units. Through this project, links were established with central governmental agencies and also with the University of Sierra Leone. The relationship between the Teachers College and the trial schools was of a hierarchical structure, rather than one of shared responsibility. The situation was characterized by its potential for collaboration, but it was not realized in practice.

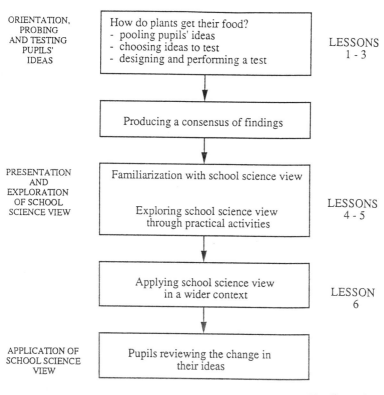

Needham 1987

Source: Needham, R. (1987). *Approaches to teaching plant nutrition*, Childrens' Learning in Science Project, Centre for Studies in Science and Mathematics Education, University of Leeds, 1987, p.10.

Figure 4.2 Outline of the plant nutrition teaching scheme

Implications

1.   The management of the school, and particularly the principal, should be aware of SBCD activities initiated by various groups and sources, and they should adequately support such initiatives.
2.   In large schools it is desirable to establish curriculum committees in which the principal should take part, but not necessarily serve as its chairman/woman.
3.   Teachers' participation in curriculum development may enhance their identification with the school and increase their feeling of belonging. Nevertheless, perseverance of teachers in jobs of this type can be ensured only if such work is duely acknowledged and remunerated. Involvement in SBCD should entitle teachers to a reduced teaching load.
4.   Schools should maintain contact with local educational authorities, and establish partnership with other schools in the same locality or in the close vicinity for the sake of co-ordinating SBCD activities. They should also co-operate with local organizations, industries and businesses by answering their needs and recruiting their help for local level curriculum development.
5.   Co-operative endeavours with local cultural institutions and partnership in curriculum development with local institutions of higher education have proved to be highly rewarding, and schools should take advantage of such opportunities.
6.   Schools should be alert to identify non-expensive local resources, which may serve as a basis for designing learning activities. People pursuing occupations related to topics dealt with within the curriculum, local institutions, etc., may enrich the relevance of externally developed curricula.
7.   Schools should establish forums which involve parents in a variety of curriculum-related decisions, and especially in incorporating issues of local interest in the school programme.
8.   In school level decision-making, as much attention   as possible should be paid to the interest revealed by students in topics of different types. Schools should establish channels through which information can be gathered, at regular time intervals, about changes in the areas of the students' interest. This information should be used in decisions about course offering and in determining rules related to elective subjects in the school.

V. Evaluating school-based curriculum development projects

Conceptually, the evaluation of school-based curriculum is no different from curriculum evaluation in general. Consequently, all models, schemes, designs, materials and approaches presented in the curriculum evaluation literature are also applicable to SBCD. Nevertheless, constraints of time, training, and resources available for the evaluation of SBCD products, in practice, necessitate some adjustment.

Curriculum development is a time-consuming endeavour. Central curriculum development teams may spend several years preparing instructional materials for a one-year course in a particular subject. In contrast, SBCD products are mostly prepared by small teams of teachers, who usually carry out curriculum development activities on a part-time basis alongside their teaching load. Curriculum development activities inside the school focus on immediate needs. Teams rarely work on a particular course of study for more than a year, and quite frequently they have to prepare materials for use in the same year of production.

The difficulties imposed by time constraints are balanced by the fact that the framework of SBCD facilitates the collection of evaluation inputs, which are the by-products of daily work in the school, such as minutes of staff conferences and what Lindvall and Cox (1970) call 'curriculum embedded tests', i.e. assignments, exercises, homework, tests given to pupils as a part of their routine school work, and also reviewed and scored by teachers as part of their own routine work.

While the professional literature includes numerous reports about the evaluation of particular SBCD programmes, very little has been done to systematize procedures or to suggest models, taking into consideration the unique evaluation conditions of SBCD.

Characteristics of SBCD which have a bearing on determining a suitable way of evaluation are, for instance, the nature of the development activity; the distance between user and developer, and whether the curriculum is for single or recurrent use.

The development activity: SBCD may mean selecting instructional materials, adapting or supplementing existing programmes for local needs, or developing new programme units or modules.

The distance between user and developer: In the context of SBCD the developer him or herself may be the user of the programme. Quite frequently, however, users did not participate in the process of the development.

Single versus recurrent use: Some SBCD products and also, but less frequently, centrally developed ones are meant to be used on a single occasion. This is the case, for example, with curriculum modules dealing with current events. Exciting technological innovations, momentous cultural events, major economic changes, or natural disasters may call for such single use.

Continuous evaluation linked to development and use

Continuous curriculum evaluation is important because of the need to carry out formative evaluation of educational programmes at the early phases of their development and because judgements about curricula and instructional materials, as about other phenomena in the field of education, have a time-bound validity.

As curriculum development initiatives became widespread, both at national and at local-level, and the sequence of actions in this multiphase endeavour was articulated, experts tried to describe evaluation activities appropriate to each phase.

In this section evaluation activities in the following three phases in the life-cycle of SBCD products will be dealt with: pre-development, the phase of programme development, and that of using the programme.

1. Pre-development phase

The need for collecting information about the context in which a particular curriculum innovation will be put to use is emphasized by most experts in the field of programme evaluation (Huberman and Cox, 1990). Stufflebeam et al. (1971) introduced the term 'context evaluation' and claimed that evaluators should gather information about needs which have not been met, missed opportunities, and problems. According to Pennington (1985), evaluation experts can provide information needed for curriculum planners by:

- analyzing relevant reports and publications;
- drawing on the perceptions, experiences and expectations of those familiar with the context, such as teachers, curriculum consultants, and would-be employers of the school leavers;
- reviewing existing curricular materials and critiques of their quality;
- utilizing results of routine achievement surveys or examinations;
- comparing the characteristics of successful textbooks with those of less successful ones, and
- organizing community forums to discuss the needs for new programmes.

2. The development phase

In the phase of programme development, evaluation focuses on examining the adequacy of programme components or elements and the sequence of learning activities. As soon as the first draft is available, the whole programme becomes the target of evaluation.

Evaluation at this phase may use empirical data collected during trialling of curriculum products or by analytical examination of the programme plan and of instructional materials. The reported findings may be accompanied by suggestions for programme revision. This may lead to iterative cycles of revision, trialling and evaluation. In practice, however, experienced teams seldom need more than a single cycle of trial and revision.

Examples of evaluation approaches used at this phase are presented below.

(1)   Learner Verification and Revision

Evaluation based on trialling of instructional materials is referred to as *Learner Verification and Revision* (EPIE, 1980). *Figure 5.1* shows the revision of a page in a draft version of a primary reader. There are substantially more correct responses for the revised exercise and illustration than for the original ones, thus proving the effectiveness of the revision.

(2)   Intrinsic evaluation

Intrinsic evaluation focuses on the inherent characteristics of curricula rather than on their effects. According to Eraut (1985), the curricular traits to be examined are those of the adequacy of the curriculum goals, consistency between goals espoused and the content of the instructional materials, and the accuracy, coverage and significance of content. Intrinsic evaluation studies frequently use evaluation checklists. An extensive collection of curriculum evaluation checklists was compiled by Woodbury (1979). An example of a checklist used by the National Study of School Evaluation (1987) to evaluate a school's mathematics programme is presented in *Table 5.1*.

(3)   Curriculum criticism

Another approach to evaluation can be found in curriculum criticism, first advocated by Mann (1969), and later developed and expanded by Eisner (1985) into an effective method for improving educational programmes. Curriculum criticism has its roots in the cognateness of instructional materials and literature.

Original Directions

Underline the man behind the man with the drum.
Circle the man in front of the man with the horn.

Revised Directions

Look below at the people who play music in the
parade. Point to the lady with the horn. Now
point to the one in front of the lady.

Point to the boy playing the drum. Now point
to the one behind the boy. Underline the one
behind the boy.

Source: EPIE. (1980). *Educational Products Information Exchange: Deciphering
LRV,* Vol. 12, p.46.

Figure 5.1 A picture and its revision

Table 5.1 Descriptive criteria of mathematics curriculum

Descriptive Criteria

1. The curriculum is consistent with the philosophy and goals of the school .... 5 4 3 2 1 na
2. The offerings extend the skills and understanding developed in previous courses ... 5 4 3 2 1 na
3. Courses at all levels stress understanding and the ability to use important mathematical relations such as equality, inequality and congruence .... 5 4 3 2 1 na
4. Courses at all levels stress understanding of and proper use of mathematical symbols . 5 4 3 2 1 na
5. Courses at all levels stress an understanding of estimation skills .... 5 4 3 2 1 na
6. Courses at all levels stress algorithmic and heuristic strategies for problem solving .. 5 4 3 2 1 na
7. Courses include the use of a calculator as an option if appropriate .... 5 4 3 2 1 na
8. Instruction in reading comprehension skills directly related to mathematics is provided at all levels of the program .... 5 4 3 2 1 na
9. The offerings include development of the real and complex number systems .... 5 4 3 2 1 na
10. Appropriate courses stress the nature of proof and provide the student with opportunities to develop competency in handling the process of proof .... 5 4 3 2 1 na

Source: National Study of School Evaluation. (1987). *Evaluative Criteria*, 6th edition, NSSE. (p.232).

Both are textual materials, usually published in the form of books or articles. Thus, for Willis (1978), evaluation:

"...is an art as well as a science. While it is well for the curriculum worker to know the scientific principles, the empirical data, and the technological applications, that inform much of his practice, it is equally well for him to be conversant with those aspects of arts which come into play, when what happens with a curriculum or in a classroom inevitably spills out beyond those scientific constructs he has chosen to employ". (p. 93).

3. Using SBCD products

School authorities are aware that SBCD needs support in terms of time allocation, access to expert consultants, resources, etc., but they believe that once the curriculum products are ready, teachers can return to their classes and devote their time to their pupils. While programme development implies co-operative work among teachers, the use of such curriculum products is considered the private task of each teacher.

In contrast to the common practice of allocating resources to the maintenance of school buildings and to hardware, school authorities overlook the maintenance needs of instructional software. SBCD products are meant to serve the needs of the school for several years, and without adequate maintenance they may quickly lose their viability.

Evaluating the use of curricula serves the purpose of identifying flaws in the maintenance of programmes and of suggesting ways which may increase the effectiveness of the continued use of the programme. Accordingly, it should focus on questions of the following types:

1. Is the programme used in the classes in a way that is consistent with the philosophy specified by its developers?

2. Does the programme continue to hold the interest of those who prepared it or use it in their classes? Is it discussed formally or informally by teachers and other school staff members? Does the school arrange open days to air problems encountered in using

the programme? Do inspectors or local authorities continue to take an interest in the success of the programme?

3.   Are there further attempts to update the programme, broaden it, supplement it, and increase the resources available? Are there opportunities for systematic in-service training activities in the use of the programme? Have teachers changed some aspects of the programme?

4.   Do pupils attain the objectives of the programme? Is there evidence for growth in cognitive, affective, and psychomotor achievements?

Monitoring SBCD at the school level

Schools may be successful in developing SBCD products of high quality yet, at the same time, the overall monitoring of curriculum development inside the school may suffer from serious shortcomings.

Several questionnaires have been developed for examining this aspect of school life (see NSSE, 1987; Metropolitan Borough of Solihull, 1980). Illustrative examples of issues mentioned in these instruments are presented below:

Democratization of planning: What arrangements are made to ensure that all teachers are involved in curriculum development of some type?

Responding to local needs: Is an opportunity given to parents, community experts, local industry representatives, and local associations and organizations to participate in decisions about the curriculum?

Institutionalization of SBCD activities: What is the scope of SBCD activities, resources, working procedures?

Care for populations of special needs: Are able children, children with learning difficulties, children with behaviour problems, specially gifted children all catered to?

Multi-ethnic programmes: Has the school an explicit policy opposing racism? What steps are taken to communicate this policy to children, parents, teaching and non-teaching staff, etc.?

Equal opportunity for boys and girls: Are all curriculum choices available to every child?

Balance in study areas: Is the curriculum biased toward academic disciplines?

Evaluation as consumer orientation

SBCD products may serve the needs of a broad group of users or only of those who participated in their development. Ensuring the 'exportability' of curriculum products has implications for both development and evaluation. Regarding development, other users will need a more complete description of the programme rationale and a more detailed set of instructions for use, than users who are also developers. This may require intensive training, and some external help in monitoring the use of the programme.

Evaluation of an 'exportable' programme entails examining the availability of supporting materials, their quality and their suitability to any particular group of recommended users.

Beyond evaluating such accessories of a programme, there is a need to provide a consumer orientation scheme which describes and, if possible, also validates its characteristics. Much attention is paid to consumer orientation in our society, and quality conscious buyers can obtain information about the merits of a wide variety of goods. Consumer orientation is also available for cultural goods. Newspapers contain evaluative information on new films, books, and television programmes. A variety of guides help teachers to select instructional materials.

Where there is a large group of users, there is a need to prepare a scheme of reviewing procedures which can be easily used. Enterprises for this purpose were initiated by national or regional institutions in several countries. Examples of centralized reviewing of SBCD products are the "National Science Teachers Association: Focus on Excellence" group in the USA (Pennick, Yager and Bonnstetter 1986) and the Secondary Science Curriculum Review, SSCR (1987) in the United Kingdom. The evaluation model of SSCR is presented in *Figure 5.2.*

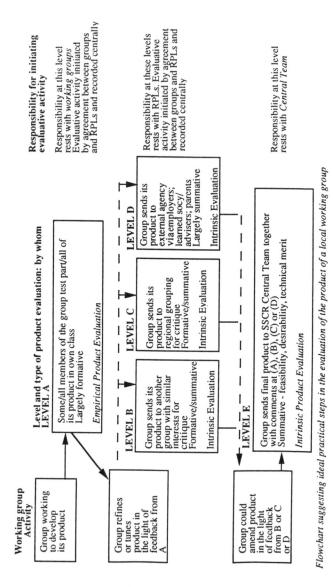

Flowchart suggesting ideal practical steps in the evaluation of the product of a local working group

Secondary Science Curriculum Review 1987

Figure 5.2 **The secondary science curriculum review evaluation scheme**

It can be seen that the evaluation is carried out at three different levels: empirical product evaluation by members of the development team; intrinsic evaluation by external reviewers from other teams engaged in similar curriculum development work, critics, and agencies of stakeholders of the programme; and intrinsic evaluation by the central team.

4. Evaluating the impact of SBCD at system level

So far, issues related to evaluating the quality of a particular SBCD programme have been examined. The procedures described in the previous sections may be of use in judging the merits of programmes, and in helping developers and users to improve their quality. But SBCD is more than a possible method of preparing curricula and instructional materials. It also represents an approach to education which supports the view that teachers should act as partners in determining the programme of their own work or the curriculum of the school they teach in.

Worldwide attempts to initiate SBCD reflect the growing confidence among educators that teachers will accept the challenge of participating in SBCD, and carry out this task successfully, that the programmes developed in this way will be high quality products, which will eventually contribute to the improvement of education. Unfortunately, these tenets have never been put to the test. Curriculum experts who favour the SBCD approach have carried out small-scale validation studies of particular programmes, but hitherto no system-level examination of these issues has been carried out.

More needs to be known about the status of SBCD in schools today for decisions to be taken about its future, its desired scope in schools of different types, the support needed for increasing its effectiveness, and adequately linking it with national or system-level curriculum frameworks. To gain such knowledge there is a need to compile a list of questions to be answered; identify types of studies which may yield valid responses and finall carry out such studies and summarize their findings.

Since the aim of this section is to suggest ways of evaluating SBCD, only the first of these issues will be discussed.

5. A framework for a SBCD data base

Data collection on SBCD is carried out mostly for a particular school, either for the purpose of accreditation (National Study of School Evaluation, 1987), or as a routine report to the educational authorities (Inner London Educational Authority, 1982). In this section a list of questions will be presented which should be answered at school level, although a summary of answers across schools rather than within a single one is supposed to provide findings which may inform decision-makers. The questions deal with the state-of-the-art of SBCD; changes in SBCD over time, quality of the SBCD product, and the outcomes of using SBCD products.

(a) State-of-the-art of SBCD in schools
1. What SBCD patterns have emerged? (Who participates, what are the working procedures?)
2. What proportions of locally and externally developed curriculum materials are used in the school? What factors are associated with the magnitude of these proportions?
3. Several types of curriculum development activities are described as SBCD, the most salient being curriculum selection adaptation, supplementing, integrating, and producing new materials. What is the proportion of each of the development types in the totality of SBCD activities?
4. Is there an ideal balance between locally and externally developed curricula? If so, what are its parameters? How are the latter determined?
5. If such an ideal pattern is identifiable, is it the same for different groups of children (age, ability level, motivation, socio-economic status, personality traits), for different teaching purposes (introducing a new topic, corrective teaching, individualized teaching, enrichment studies), and for different subject areas?

(b) Changes over time in the status of SBCD
6. What changes have occurred in the status of SBCD in the school during the last five or ten years? Has the scope of SBCD increased or decreased? Has its focus changed? Have development procedures changed?

7. Provide details of the history of individual teachers' involvement in SBCD. Have they exhibited perseverance? What factors are associated with perseverance in participating in SBCD?
8. For how long have particular SBCD products been used in the school? What changes have they undergone, if any?
   (c) The quality of the SBCD product
9. What is the quality of the SBCD product on the basis of intrinsic product evaluation criteria? Compare its quality with commercially or institutionally prepared materials.
10. Were the curriculum products evaluated? By whom? What model, method, etc. of evaluation was used? What were the results of the evaluation?
   (d) The impact of using SBCD products
11. Have the SBCD products affected teachers' performance? Have the products promoted 'curriculum literacy' (i.e. a better understanding of the nature of curriculum or instructional materials; greater precision in describing personal experiences, selecting criteria for evaluation, and using them)?
12. Do teachers identify more with the school and with a particular educational programme? (Is it good that teachers identify with a self-developed programme rather than critically examine it continually?)
13. Has the SBCD activity contributed to improving the school climate in terms of cohesion, co-operation, initiative, tolerance to criticism, and general quality of life?
14. Do children using SBCD products like their school better, and carry out school assignments or homework better than those using externally produced programmes?
15. Do children have a different attitude to SBCD products than to commercially or institutionally produced ones? Do SBCD products take better care of individual differences than other types of programmes?
16. Do children acquire a higher level of mastery of skills and contents through SBCD products than through externally developed products?

Large-scale national and cross-national studies on the impact of home environment variables and school-related organizational and teaching behaviours on affective and cognitive educational variables, have provided a basis on which to interpret the findings of any particular school-based study (Walker, 1976; Coleman, 1966). Thus, for example, having information about the correlation across the whole educational system between any two variables may help in interpreting empirical findings related to the correlation between these two variables in a particular school-based study.

The same principle applies to the issue of SBCD. In the absence of basic information about trends in the entire educational system, references to small-scale school-based studies may yield biased and deceptive information about the significance of SBCD and about its potential contribution to education.

Implications

1.   SBCD evaluation should aim at three targets:
   • Products developed by local teams
   • School level activities related to SBCD
   • Changes at national level as a result of supporting SBCD
2.   Evaluators of a particular SBCD product shoud examine its quality, the way it is used and its impact.
3.   Despite the differences in the scope of activites related to, and resources available for national and school-based curriculum development, conceptually, evaluation of SBCD products is not different from that of other curriculum products. Therefore, models and methods suitable for evaluating educational products in general, can be used also for evaluating school-based curricula.
4.   Needs assessment studies examining the nature and the quality of available curriculum materials, local needs and demands, pre-requisite knowledge and interest of the target population, should preceed decisions about the parameters of any locally developed educational programme.
5.   Evaluators of SBCD programmes should conveniently take advantage of 'curriculum embedded products', i. e. products generated during the process of development and routine use of the curriculum (like reaction of teachers and pupils to instructional materials, work assignments, homework, test and examinations administered in the class), as input for evaluation. Consequently,

they should have easily access to a large quantity of non-reactive evaluation data.

6.   As to school level activities, evaluation should deal with questions like democratization of SBCD or providing opportunity for all interested teachers to participate, involvement of the parents and community members in curriculum related decisions, adequate maintenance and renewal of SBCD products.

7.   Finally, at national level, evaluation should examine the reaction of schools to the challenge of SBCD, their perseverance in producing school-based curricula, the factors associated with effective SBCD, and the contribution of SBCD to the improvement of education.

VI. Arguments for and against school-based curriculum development

The professional literature is replete with arguments supporting school-based curriculum development. Most publications dealing with this topic have a hortative undertone. Very few articles representing adversary views of SBCD have been published. Experts who oppose SBCD favouring centralistic curriculum development and supporting the 'scientific' approach have advertently avoided polemics with supporters of SBCD. Nor have they attempted to describe their view of the weaknesses of SBCD. They have confined themselves to specifying successful patterns of co-operation between experts in subject areas, curriculum, and social studies, and have suggested designs for scholarly studies to be carried out in conjunction with developing school programmes. Although arguments against SBCD may be implied in their writing, they have seldom made them explicit. Arguments against SBCD are in fact mostly contained in the caveats of writers sympathetic to SBCD.

This chapter reviews the arguments for and against SBCD. It should be borne in mind that by 1990 the heated debate between the advocates of SBCD and those of the centralistic approach has considerably abated. Once it was recognized that both the centralistic and the school-based (or local) modes of curriculum development had a contribution to make , the point of the debate shifted from repudiating one or another model to striking a balance between them.

Thus some argue for limiting the intervention of central authorities and agencies to the establishment of a national curriculum framework, as reflected in the following words of Holt (1987).

"What I am suggesting therefore is that the development of major curriculum initiatives which require comprehensive review and consultation in order to achieve an acceptable coherence of context, pedagogy, materials and assessment be left to curriculum development teams which are not school-based. .... Teachers in school would be encouraged to see their role in the partnership of curriculum development as that of intelligent and informed critic-cum-researcher ..... and to make adjustments that take account of the impact of local conditions that only they can fully comprehend". (p. 82)

Others support strong involvement of central bodies such as educational authorities, research and development institutions and private publishing companies, in prescribing the major parameters of the school programmes and producing instructional materials, with schools deciding only about a limited part of the total programme.

It should be remembered that SBCD is a generic term describing a variety of non-centralist curriculum development patterns. Therefore it may well be that certain of the arguments listed below apply only to a sub-category of the SBCD mode.

Arguments for SBCD

Arguments in favour of SBCD take into account socio-political ideals, the definition of the teacher's role, local needs orientation, and effective monitoring and control.

1. Socio-political ideals

The right of self-determination is one of the dominant ideals of contemporary political thought. Not surprisingly it has affected life in school, too. In numerous educational systems attempts have been made to endow schools with autonomy in matters of the curriculum.

The implications of school autonomy for SBCD need further clarification. *Firstly*, in whom does the autonomy reside? Are the teachers acting as substitutes for parents? Should the members or the representatives of the community be involved in making decisions about the curriculum? What is the role of the principal in implementing the school's autonomy in the area of curriculum development? Strong leadership in the school may facilitate SBCD, but the principal's intervention may infringe on the right of self-determination of others. Secondly, in practice, is the right of self-determination realized by the school-based groups dealing with the curriculum? Gordon (1987) examines teachers' perception of the school's autonomy and finds that despite formal declarative statements about autonomy, teachers believe that they are constrained in making decisions about the curriculum.

2. Role definition of teachers

Two aspects of the teacher's role definition have bearings on SBCD: responsibility for the curriculum and the status of the teaching profession.

(1) *Responsibility for the curriculum:* The curriculum movement of the 1950s favoured highly structured educational programmes providing teachers with detailed instructions. The most common criterion for successful use of the programme was adherence to these instructions, that is 'fidelity of implementation'. When teachers failed or were unwilling to fully carry out the instructions with a high level of fidelity, in spite of intensive in-service training, it was concluded that in order to implement an educational programme well, teachers must themselves gain experience in programme development. This was not to say that teachers should develop all programmes or instructional materials they used, but that 'curriculum literacy' was seen as a prerequisite for successful programme implementation, and such literacy could be acquired only through active participation in the development of some educational programmes.

(2) *The status of the teaching profession:* Traditionally, teaching, especially in primary school, has not been considered an area of professional expertise, and teachers have not been considered a professional group. Unlike the education of lawyers, doctors and engineers, that of teachers has not traditionally taken place in a framework of recognized academic status. Moreover, the teaching

profession offers very little career opportunities for those who excel in their work. Only a small proportion of teachers are promoted to school principal or inspector, and the qualifications needed for such positions are quite different from those needed for succeeding in teaching. In the 1970s and 1980s efforts were made in several countries on behalf of teachers' unions in conjunction with the national educational authorities to raise the status of teachers and transform teaching into a professional career area. One manifestation of professionalization is the provision of career opportunities based on responsibility. Another manifestation is the opportunity of gaining public recognition for creative innovations.

The involvement of teachers in curriculum development may contribute to their professionalization in two ways. Firstly, it may provide a basis for promotion. Thus the position of 'curriculum postholders' was introduced in England and Wales (Campbell 1985). Secondly, teachers appointed for such positions may gain public recognition for rendering special professional services to their schools and through contributing to the improvement of the educational practice, in general.

3. Local-needs orientation

SBCD is in a better position to respond to local needs than a nationally developed curriculum. It can take into consideration the unique characteristics of the ecosystem of a particular area, the cultural and religious values of the local population, occupational opportunities for school leavers, and the ability level of the schoolgoers together with their previous learning experiences and the resources available in and to the school.

Reid (1987) states that responding to differential local needs from a single national center may be an unmanageable task, while at local level such problems can be more easily solved:

"When education systems are centrally administered, curriculum development or organisational change tends to be seen as a 'one-off' exercise. Plans have to be made and resources gathered for a major co-ordinated effort to bring matters to a successful conclusion.... Thus, planning and implementing change is seen as a costly exercise that can only be undertaken infrequently. But at the school level the scale is different, the opportunities and constraints are of a different order. Teachers 'know' their schools, their children and their communities in a way that central authorities can never 'know' the national systems they administer". (p. 111)

4. *Effective monitoring and control*

One of the arguments in favour of SBCD is that it allows effectiveness in monitoring the programme and controlling resources. Schools are more stable institutions than curriculum developing agencies. Numerous centrally produced educational programmes continue to be used in schools at a time when the development agencies have already been disbanded. Schools can adapt programmes to changing conditions, and update them if necessary.

Arguments against SBCD

Some of the arguments presented above point out the merits of SBCD, but call attention to its limitations at the same time. Thus, they also may be used as arguments against exaggerated demands for fully rejecting national intervention in the curriculum and using only school-based curriculum materials.

For the sake of balance, the arguments presented in this section focus on the disadvantages of determining all parameters of the curriculum at the school level and of using only school-based instructional materials. These arguments do not deny to the school the role of autonomous partner in the process of determining some components of its own curriculum.

5. *The teachers' ability to produce curriculum*

Naturally the situation may vary from one country to another but it is reasonable to believe that some teachers can and will produce teaching materials. There is evidence that many of them actually do work of this kind, but no information is available about the proportion of teachers who are interested in or able to do such work. Of course, one can train teachers for this purpose, but the question is, on account of what? Should this engagement be a high priority component of teacher training?

There are signs that the feasibility of such accomplishments is doubtful. *First*, there is little hope that the teaching profession will in the forthcoming years attract candidates of high intellectual capabilities. On the contrary, it is more likely that in competition with other more prestigious and better paid professions it will lose such candidates. *Second*, large-scale engagement of teachers in developing instructional materials will necessarily require increased expenditure and there are good reasons to doubt whether society will be willing to bear these expenses. *Third*, educational technology will increasingly intrude on the field of education and bring about a proliferation of commercially produced instructional materials. In the face of these observable trends the odds are against massive involvement of teachers in producing instructional materials.

6. *The quality of the product*

Some teaching materials developed by teachers excel in their quality, but most do not match the quality of materials developed by professional curriculum teams. If one considers the vast amount of items that curriculum teams screen until they select a single one for inclusion in a teaching programme, one must seriously question whether teachers can do such a job. Obtaining access to authentic materials which are used by curriculum experts in the process of their work is, in most cases, impossible for individual teachers. Of course, experts in various subjects can co-operate in the process of school-based curriculum development but, in practice, national curriculum projects find it difficult to obtain help from highly qualified experts -- so how can one expect that individual schools will be able to create such links?

7. *The professional role definition of the teacher*

The SBCD idea reflects the presupposition that curriculum construction and the development of teaching materials constitute an essential element of the teacher's role. This may be so, but no attempt has been made empirically to validate the presupposition. It may also be the case that the capacities for teaching and for constructing teaching materials are not related to each other. Even if one endorses the view that teachers have to be familiar with the principles of developing teaching materials and accept that they should have some experience in doing such work, it does not necessarily mean that they should systematically and constantly be engaged in such work. Imposing the task of materials development upon the teacher will reduce the time available for carrying out other school activities which cannot be delegated.

8. *The characteristics of teacher-initiated changes*

An argument frequently adduced in favour of SBCD is that the reform intentions of outside planners become diluted when implemented in schools. Supporters of SBCD contend that teachers are more effective in dealing with programmes developed by themselves than in implementing changes suggested by others. This may be true, but the changes initiated by teachers tend to be limited in scope and, being usually based on consensually accepted educational ideas, are conservative in nature.

Most school-based innovations touch on marginal aspects of educational programmes. The implementation of major curriculum changes is greatly facilitated by being monitored by the central educational authorities. The provision of in-service training opportunities, the establishment of adequately equipped resource centers, and the continuous availability of consulting services are necessary for effective implementation of large scale changes.

Thus, it is highly unlikely that radical change can occur in the school programme without intervention of the central educational authorities.

9. *Weak evaluation basis*

SBCD programmes tend to have a weak evaluation basis. Despite the fact that most SBCD projects have an evaluation component, these evaluation components can hardly provide a firm basis for judging the quality of programmes. *Firstly*, schools do not have well trained evaluation experts. *Secondly*, teachers involved in development activities do not attribute high importance to evaluation. Frequently teachers do not have the time to carry out programme evaluation in a systematic manner after having devoted much time and energy to planning the change and implementing it. Campbell (1985) reviewed the evaluation of ten SBCD curriculum projects and found that in only five cases did the entire staff of the school participate in the evaluation; only in two development projects were the school principal and the curriculum co-ordinator involved in evaluating the programme.

10. *A common core of knowledge*

Societies are characterized by sharing a basic set of concepts, ideas, literary allusions, and characters from history, and the socialization of the individual implies becoming familiar with them. Hirsch (1987) compiled a list of approximately 3000 items and referred to them as basic knowledge in Cultural Literacy. Stating that the items differed from one culture to another, he subtitled the book "What every American has to know". Hirsch claimed that concepts like relativity and photosynthesis, geographical locations like Hiroshima and literary quotations like "To be or not to be" constituted, at least in the USA, and quite likely in many literate cultures across the world, a part of a literate person's basic vocabulary. Without familiarity with these items one cannot well understand one's own language.

The list compiled by Hirsch contains items from a great variety of subjects taught in schools. One may disagree with him in the scope of the items or the validity of his selection. One may even judge the attempt as an arbitrary exercise lacking any worth. Nevertheless, in most countries importance is attached to imparting knowledge about the national cultural heritage. A national curriculum framework would seem to be more effective in attaining this goal than SBCD.

Content bias in national examinations

A national syllabus, even if it permits school-based choices from alternative content-blocks, may serve as a basis for planning content-fair examinations for all schools of the nation. In contrast, widespread SBCD activities in any educational system lead to the diversification of curriculum contents taught in schools, therefore creating difficulties in preparing nationally valid examinations. Problems related to content bias of tests were examined by Walker and Schaffarzick (1977), and the authors demonstrated that the majority of tests are biased toward one or another curriculum, and they lack cross-curricular content validity.

Educational systems with a tradition of SBCD have made numerous attempts to ensure that tests used in the whole system are content-fair. Three of such attempts made in England and Wales, which may serve as a model for other countries, will be described here.

1.   The *Assessment of Performance Unit* (APU) carried out large-scale testing in schools of England and Wales, and to avoid content-bias they developed tests which focused on what they defined as a 'development line' in a particular area of study (such as mathematical, scientific, language, etc.), rather than on the mastery of pre-specified content units. Areas of study were not defined in terms of subjects taught in schools, since it was claimed that whatever the range of subject matters taught, and whatever the differences in content across curricula used, everything contributes to one or more of these lines of development. As indicated by Pring (1981):

"The procedure adopted by APU was to establish working groups for each of the lines of development'. These groups would identify the main strand of development which would reflect the curriculum aims and activities of schools - whatever the balance of subjects and differences in curriculum content between one school and another". (p.157).

2. The attempt of school-based profiling constitutes another example of carrying out curriculum-free evaluation of educational achievement. Teachers were asked to provide profile description of their students, which contained specification of areas studies in which the individual participated and assessment of his or her level of achievement. To enable comparison across schools, there was a need to establish standards of both the curricula used and the achievement levels attained (Murphy and Torrance 1988).

3. The most comprehensive framework for carrying out national examinations in the face of diversity of curricula used in the schools can be attributed to the Waddell (1978) committee of England and Wales. The committee recommended that examining-boards should legitimize three examination modes in each subject-matter according to the following patterns:

Mode I. Examinations conducted by the examining board on syllabuses set and published by the board.

Mode II. Examination conducted by the examining board on syllabuses devised by individual schools and/or groups of schools, and approved by the board.

Mode III. Examination set and marked internally by individual schools or groups of schools, but moderated by the board, on syllabuses devised by individual schools or groups of schools.

The allowance made to use *Mode II* and *Mode III* examinations guarantees the school's autonomy in matters of curriculum, and moderation on behalf of examining boards. This entails controlling the standards of the questions and the grades assigned to a particular examination paper, enabling comparisons across schools.

SBCD within a national curriculum framework

The arguments presented for and against SBCD reflect the view that these two phenomena, the SBCD and the National Curriculum Framework complement each other with each fulfilling a unique role in determining what should be taught in schools. Towards the end of the 1980s one could observe a reconciliation between these two approaches. Educational systems which previously gave full freedom to schools introduced a national curriculum framework to guide schools in organizing their programme. The movement towards disseminating SBCD in highly centralized educational systems has been slow, but its importance as complementary to national curriculum development has been universally acknowledged.

By 1990, most educational systems made decisions about curriculum both at national and local levels, although the scope of SBCD activities is quite negligible in a great many of them. It should be noted that developing and introducing a national curriculum framework, in a country which in the past bestowed full autonomy upon the schools, is easier than introducing or increasing the scope of SBCD activities in a highly centralized educational system. This is so, because a single institution may create, disseminate and monitor a loosely prescribed national curriculum framework with a relatively high level of success, while the implementation of SBCD across an educational system implies re-educating all teachers and considerably changing teacher education programmes. The transition towards SBCD requires time and can be realized only phase by phase. Using the term coined by Havelock and Huberman(1977), the 'scale of change' of such transition is large. Numerous components of the system have to be changed (like the conditions of textbook publication, provision of learning resources, teacher education programmes, supervision, examination system), and radical changes in the behaviour of persons implementing the transition are required.

The proliferation of SBCD in an educational system has two dimensions: the scope of curriculum coverage and the scope of schools in which SBCD activities take place. As for the scope of curriculum coverage, in most countries which recently adopted the idea of SBCD, schools were challenged to assume responsibility for developing a specified proportion of their programme (usually 10-30 per cent). In most cases the specified proportion sets an upper limit of permissible SBCD activities. In reality, however, SBCD activities seldom approach this upper limit. The second dimension of proliferation is the proportion of schools in which SBCD activities take place. Even in countries with a long tradition of SBCD, no quantitative information is available about the proportion of schools seriously engaged in such activities, let alone about the nature of these. The scope of SBCD activities in a particular country, as well as in a particular study area, can be described in terms of these two dimensions.

In the face of slow progress of proliferating SBCD across and within educational systems, one may ask whether SBCD is a suitable approach for all systems and all schools. Are there pre-conditions which should be met in order to advise systems or individual schools getting involved in SBCD activities? Should developing countries be encouraged to allow SBCD activities in the nation's schools? Should they encourage such activities? Is the above specified balance of advantages and disadvantages of SBCD in developing countries identical to that observed in highly industrialized countries?

Undoubtedly, SBCD can be more easily implemented in educational systems with highly qualified and well-educated teachers, who work in well-equipped schools, with small classes, and are entitled to a reduced teaching load, or even being fully released from teaching assignment for a specified period of time, in compensation for SBCD services rendered to the school. Such conditions are seldom found in educational systems of developing countries. Consequently, the chances for successful SBCD activities are less than those in highly industrialized ones. Yet, in spite of the scarcity of resources, educational developments across the world at the beginning of the last decade of our millennium do not justify discouraging developing countries from SBCD activities and experimentations. Hitherto, as described in more detail in the previous sections, evidence has been accumulated about successful attempts of introducing SBCD activities in developing countries (Clarken 1990; Ekanayake 1990; Okpala and Onocha 1988; Sutaria 1990). These instances are encouraging, and it is worthwhile to continue to support additional endeavours of this type.

Nevertheless, it would be a mistake to present successful attempts of SBCD in highly industrialized countries as a model for the developing countries. SBCD activities in developing countries should be different from those in industrialized ones, at least along three dimensions: the scope of their proliferation; the type of SBCD activities; and the pattern of monitoring such activities.

The scope of proliferation: In developing countries it is desirable to limit the scope of curriculum coverage for which SBCD activities are recommended. A reasonable starting point may be 10 per cent of the curriculum, which gradually may be expanded up to 25 per cent. Also, the scope of schools participating in such enterprises should initially be limited, and gradually expanded after providing suitable training for teachers. Significant benefits can be derived for the educational system even if only a few schools carry out SBCD activities. Involvement of a few teachers in activities may set the standard for the whole system and may constitute an avenue for promotion along the professional ladder.

The type of SBCD activities: As reported in the professional literature SBCD activities in developing countries are frequently linked to rural development programmes. SBCD activities are elements of comprehensive programmes which aim to contribute to the quality of life and not only to the educational achievement of the students. They enjoy strong community support. Frequently, they are carried out as a co-operative enterprise of several schools and are supported by a regional Teacher College or University. Some of the projects focus on producing remedial or corrective teaching materials. There are few instances of producing alternative sets of instructional materials. The instructional materials produced at local level supplement national curriculum units rather than producing entirely new courses.

The pattern of monitoring SBCD: In developing countries most SBCD activities are initiated by agents operating outside the school. Regional educational offices and/or international organizations are most frequently the initiators of SBCD projects. The production of school-based materials is assisted and supervised by experts. Also, National Curriculum Development Centers monitor SBCD activities, partly by preparing exemplary units and partly by organizing workshops in which theoretical and practical aspects of SBCD are discussed. In most developing countries the National Curriculum Framework and limited SBCD activities are not conceived as alternative ways of action, but rather as complementary.

Nevertheless, progress in this direction, in most centralized educational systems is restricted to a few experimental schools. In those countries where schools were challenged to assume responsibility for a certain proportion of their programme (mostly 10-30 per cent), one may observe more SBCD activities, but they seldom fully cover the permitted range of such actions. Most frequently such activities, limited to certain weekly hours of the school schedule, are used for augmenting the scope of studies in the core subjects. By 1990, in most educational systems where SBCD has gained a publicly recognized status, it still affects only a very small proportion of schools, and even here mostly in the selection of programmes rather than in the production of new ones. However, schools engaged in SBCD are frequently considered to belong to the nation's most prestigious schools.

Implications

1. National concern for the school programme manifested through establishing an overall curriculum framework may promote rather than hinder SBCD.
2. The national curriculum should make provision for local-level curriculum development, determine its nature and scope, provide guidelines and maintain support services for continuously raising the standards of school-based and locally- developed programmes.
3. Educational systems should develop and publish formally approved curriculum frameworks for ensuring that all pupils acquire a common core of knowledge.
4. Major curriculum initiatives requiring large scale planning and co-ordination can be better carried out by expert teams, while catering for local needs can be better accomplished through local or school level development activities.
5. Initiators of SBCD activities should be aware of the scope of resources at their disposition and plan their agenda accordingly.
6. Experience in curriculum development should be considered a useful component of pre-service and in-service teacher education

programmes. Involvement in curriculum development helps teachers to understand curriculum documents and successfully use curriculum materials developed by others.

7. Teachers interested in curriculum development should be encouraged and supported by the school while keeping in mind that excellence in teaching is not necessarily associated with excellence in curriculum development.

8. Involvement in curriculum development should be considered one of the professional promotion tracks offered to teachers.

9. The appropriate balance between externally and locally developed curricula differs across educational systems and across schools within a single system. The maximal scope of SBCD activities should be determined at the system level, and their range should be approximately 10-25 per cent of the total curriculum. Only schools with properly trained staff members and well-equipped resource centers should strive to expand their SBCD activities to reach the nationally permitted limit.

10. Since SBCD leads towards the diversification of contents taught in schools, provisions should be made for parallel diversification of the examination forms. The national examining boards should take care of moderating the standards across examinations conducted on different syllabuses.

VII. National framework and school-based development

Contemporary curriculum development is characterized by a high level of freedom bestowed upon the schools to initiate innovations within the limits of a nationally prescribed, broad curriculum framework. This approach is well articulated in the curriculum guidelines of the *Scottish Consultative Council on the Curriculum* (SCCC), the principal advisory body on the school curriculum of the Secretary of State for Scotland. A document published in 1989 describes the curriculum in relation to national, local and individual levels.

The National Curriculum Framework offers a broad range of courses to the schools. For several subject areas, guidelines and course materials emanating from the SCCC and other sources are widely used. Nationally approved full courses, short courses and modules are also available within this framework. The courses are supplemented by support materials prepared under the auspices of SCCC and other agencies.

The central education authorities assist schools in adapting the national guidelines to local circumstances. From the national curricular framework each school selects, adapts, and develops courses and modules; and from these it derives programmes appropriate to local and school needs, which are compatible with the availability of staff and resources.

At the school level there is a process of negotiation involving school, parents and pupils through which, and within local provision, a programme appropriate to needs and aspirations of each individual pupil is constructed. This programme is expected to be related to the individuals career intentions.

Examining the partnership between the central educational authorities and the school, through the perspective of the teacher's involvement in curricular decisions, reveals that the teacher's curriculum-related decisions may represent various levels of autonomy. The teacher may act as an autonomous consumer selecting from programmes specified in the national curriculum framework. He or she may adapt an available set of instructional materials or develop his or her own one. The teacher may also develop an optional course and assume responsibility for preparing both the syllabus and the instructional materials.

Curriculum experts nowadays are no longer disposed to view one or another pattern of curriculum production as a panacea for all problems encountered in dealing with school programmes. There is an increased awareness of the unique contribution to the school life of each of these decision-making and production patterns. The major concern of curriculum experts is to decide about the balance between these different approaches, under what circumstances should one prefer one pattern to another, and how could the products of the national and the school-based curriculum development be improved.

Ideally, each school should use both externally and locally produced curricula, while each teacher should be engaged in selection, adaptation, integration of curriculum materials and the production of new ones. But the ideal balance among programmes and activities of different types may vary from school-to-school, from subject-to-subject, and from teacher-to-teacher.

The appropriate balance between centrally and locally produced curricula in highly industrialized countries may be unlike that of developing countries. In the latter, at the initial phases of introducing SBCD, it may be desirable to limit its coverage to approximately 10 per cent of the total curriculum which can then be gradually augmented up to 25 per cent. This seems to be the suitable scope of SBCD activities in industrialized countries, too. But while in industrialized countries, from the very beginning the great majority of schools may be engaged in SBCD activities, in developing countries, first, only a small proportion of schools -- usually the best equipped and most prestigious ones, and those that are assisted by external agencies -- will start carrying out SBCD activities, and the spread of this practice will be highly dependent on the pace of appropriate teacher training.

It is quite likely, for instance, that local history, environmental topics, local cultural and economic resources are best studied through school-based curricula, while mathematics, foreign languages, national or world history and grammar are more amenable for treatment through a national curriculum framework. Nevertheless, national guidelines may serve as a useful framework for developing school-based programmes on topics of local interest, and local supplementation of nationally developed programmes may increase their relevance for the pupils of a particular school. Also, it may well be that some teachers prefer using programmes developed by external experts, while other teachers enjoy developing curricula for their class, and teach best using instructional materials developed by themselves. But all teachers have to acquire basic skills both in producing curricula and in using curricula produced by others. This is so because teachers frequently face the need of responding quickly to current events at the school, local, national and inter-national level, and of teaching topics for which no instructional materials have yet been developed. On the other hand, no teacher has sufficient time and knowledge for being fully self-sufficient in matters of curriculum supply.

The question of improving the quality of SBCD was addressed by Sabar (1983). In her view, the success of SBCD is dependent on the support provided by the central bodies of the national educational system, the institutions of teacher education and the schools.

National authorities need to establish a network of curriculum consultants, to set up a national information center and to make arrangements with the public examination systems to prepare suitable examination alternatives for those who use locally developed programmes.

The teacher education institutions should teach curriculum planning as an integral part of pre-service and in-service education programmes. Schools should allocate resources such as equipment, manpower, space and time for carrying out SBCD work.

The diversification of curricula used in schools may jeopardize the content validity or the curriculum-fairness of nationally produced examinations. Therefore, the intensification of SBCD requires making adequate adjustments in the national examination system for the schools.

One way of dealing with this issue is adopting the recommendations of the Waddell (1978) Committee of England and Wales, and imposing upon the national or regional examining boards so that they should conduct examinations on syllabuses devised by schools or groups of schools and also to serve as a moderator of examinations conducted at the school level, i. e. control the standards of examination questions and the grades assigned to a particular response. Indeed in numerous educational systems this approach has been successfully adopted and SBCD programmes have been allowed to conduct their own examinations under the careful monitoring and moderating of the central authorities.

Curriculum development is described by Schwab (1971) as a practical activity based on the art of the eclectic. In reality, however, the professional literature dealing with SBCD and its relation to the national curriculum framework is not sufficiently anchored in practical wisdom. It is either normative and persuasive or anecdotal. There is a dearth of relevant practical knowledge. It should be hoped that the increased interest in this topic will result in the accumulation of knowledge of this type.

Bibliography

ACEID (Asian Centre of Educational Innovation for Development) 1990. "Developing new teacher competencies in response to mega-trends in curricula", *ACEID Newsletter, Issue 36.*

Armbruster, B.B. ; Anderson, T.H. 1981. *Content area textbooks,* Washington, DC: National Institute of Education, ERIC.

Aziz, A.A. Ahmad, S.H. ; Bakar, F.A. 1990. *Improving the quality of education: strategies for implementing change,* Kuala Lumpur, Ministry of Education.

Banya, Kingsley, 1989. *Education for rural development: myth or reality,* International Journal on Educational Development, 9(2):111-26.

Berger, Eugenia Hepworth. 1987. *Parents as partners in education: the school and home working together,* 2nd edition, Columbus: Merrill Publishing Company.

Berliner, David. 1982. *The executive function of teaching.* Paper presented at AERA meeting, New York.

Blum, A. ; Kragelund, Z. ; Pottenger, F. 1981. *Development and evaluation of a curriculum adaptation scheme,* Science Education 65:521-536.

Braybrook, D. ; Lindblom, C.E. 1963. *A strategy of decision: policy evaluation as a social process,* New York: Free Press.

117

Campbell, R.J., 1985. *Developing the primary school curriculum*, London: Holt Education.

Clarken, R.H., 1990. *Conceptualizing a junior secondary social studies program for Botswana*, Paper presented at the April 16-20 annual meeting of American Educational Research Association (AERA), Boston, MA.

Coleman, J. 1966. *Report on equality of educational opportunity*, Washington, DC, US Government Printing Office.

Connelly, F.M. 1972. *The functions of curriculum development*, Interchange, 3(2-3):161-177.

Connelly, F.M. ; Clandinin, D. Jean. 1988. *Teachers as curriculum planners: narratives of experience*, New York: Teachers College Press.

De Bevoise, Wynn, 1986. *Collaboration: some principles of bridgework*, Ed. Lead. 43(5):9-12.

Ecker, D. 1985. "Theories of educational organization: modern", In T. Husén and T.N. Postlethwaite (editors): *International Encyclopedia of Education.*

Eisner, E.W. 1985. *The educational imagination: on the design and evaluation of school programs*, 2nd edition, New York: MacMillan.

Ekanayake, S.B. 1990. "Rural pedagogy: a grassroots approach to rural development". In *Prospects*, 20(1):115-127.

EPIE, 1980. *Educational products information exchange: deciphering LRV*, volume 12(3).

Eraut, M., 1985. "Intrinsic evaluation", In T. Husén and T.N. Postlethwaite (editors): *International Encyclopedia of Education.*

Evans, Dylis, M., 1989. *A small oral history project in four rural Cumbrian primary schools*, Teaching History, no. 56:25-27.

Fitzgerald, Maureen, 1990. "Education for sustainable development: decision-making for environmental education in Ethiopia", *International Journal of Educational Development*, volume 10 (4):289-302.

Glatthorn, A.A. ; Foshay, A.W. 1985. "Curriculum integration", In T. Husén and T. N. Postlethwaite (editors.): *International Encyclopedia of Education.*

Goldhammer, K. 1985. "Governance of primary and secondary education". In T. Husén and T.N. Postlethwaite (editors.): *International Encyclopedia of Education.*

Good, C.V. 1973. Dictionary of Education, 3rd edition. New York: McGraw Hill.

Goodlad, J.I. ; Klein, M. F. ; Tye, K.A., 1979. "The domains of curriculum and their study". In: Goodlad J. I. and Associates, *Curriculum inquiry: the study of curriculum practice*, New York: McGraw-Hill

Gordon, David, 1987. "Autonomy is more than just the absence of external constraints". In N. Sabar et al (eds.): *Partnership and autonomy.*

Graham, Eric, J. 1988. "Local history studies in the classroom", *Teaching History*, no. 53:25-33.

Griffith, A.D. 1990. "Social studies for nation building", *The Social Studies*, 81(4):161-5.

Grobman, A. B. ; Blum, A. 1985. "Curriculum Adaptation", In T. Husén and T.N. Postlethwaite (editors.): *International Encyclopedia of Education.*

Hargreaves, Andy, 1989. *Curriculum and assessment reform,* Milton Keynes: Open University.

Harlen, Wynne, 1985. "Science education: primary school programs". In T. Husén and T.N. Postlethwaite (editors.): *International Encyclopedia of Education.*

Havelock, R.G. ; Huberman, A.M. 1977. *Solving educational problems: a theory and reality of innovations in developing countries,* Paris: UNESCO.

Hirsch, E.D. 1987. *Cultural literacy,* Boston: Houghton Mifflin.

Holmes, B. 1977. *Science education: cultural borrowing and comparative research,* Stud. Sc. Educ. 4:83-110.

Holmes, M. 1989. "Ethical issues in curriculum". In T. Husén and T. N. Postlethwaite (editors.): *International Encyclopedia of Education,* Supplement no.1.

Holt, Maurice. 1987. "Are schools capable of making critical decisions about their curriculum". In N. Sabar; J. Rudduck and W. Reid (editors.): *Partnership and Autonomy.*

Huberman, M. ; Cox, P. 1990. "Evaluation utilization: building links between action and reflection". In *Studies in Educational Evaluation,* 16(1):157-180.

Hulbert, Louise. 1987. Health based physical education: the need to involve parents. In *Bulletin of Physical Education.,* 23(2):6-11.

Husén, T. and Postlethwaite, T.N. (editors.), 1985. *International Encyclopedia of Education,* Oxford: Pergamon Press.

Husén, T. and Postlethwaite, T.N. (editors.), 1989. *International Encyclopedia of Education: Suppl. no. 1,* Oxford: Pergamon Press.

ILEA, (Inner London Educational Authority), 1982. *Keeping the school under review*, London:ILEA.

Kim, H. 1975. "Evaluation of the mastery learning project in Korea". In *Studies in Educational Evaluation*, 1(1):13-22.

Lindvall, C.M. ; Cox, R. 1970. *The IPI evaluation program*, Chicago: Rand McNally.

Lundgren, U.P. 1972. *Frame factors and the teaching process: a contribution to curriculum theory and theory of teaching*, Stockholm: Almqvist and Wiksell.

MacDonald, J.B. 1986. "The domain of curriculum", *Journal of Curriculum and Supervision*, 1(3):205-14.

McGowan, M.T. ; Williams, R.O. 1990. *Communication within school-university partnership and its effect on curricular change*, Paper at AERA, Boston.

Mann, J.S. 1969. *Curriculum criticism, curriculum theory network*, Issue 2, Winter, p.2-14, also in Willis, G (ed): *Qualitative Evaluation*.

Martin, David, S. ; Saif, Philip, S. ; Thiel, Linda, 1987. *Curriculum development: who is involved and how?* Ed. Leadership, 44(4):40-48.

Menck, Peter. 1989. "Curriculum development in FRG: Tradition or reform?", *Education*, (Biannual collection - published by the Institute for Scientific Co-operation, Tubingen), Volume 40:49-63.

Metropolitan Borough of Solihull Education Committee, 1980. *Evaluating the primary school*, Solihull Education Authority.

Muckle, J. 1988. *A guide to soviet curriculum*, London: Croom Helm.

Murphy, R. ; Torrance, H. 1988. *The changing face of educational assessment*, Milton Keynes, Open University.

National Commission on Education, 1977. *Education for Kagisano*: Report of the National Commission on Education, Gaborone, Government Printer.

National Council of Educational Research and Training (CCERT), 1970. *Preparation and evaluation of textbooks in English*, New Delhi: NCERT.

National Study of School Evaluation, 1987, *Evaluative Criteria*. 6th edition NSSE.

Needham, R. 1987. *Teaching strategies for developing understanding in science*, University of Leeds, Centre for studies in science and mathematics education, Children's Learning in Science Project (CLISP).

Needham, R. 1987. *Approaches to teaching plant nutrition*, University of Leeds, Centre for studies in science and mathematics education, Children's Learning in Science Project (CLISP).

Nordin, A. B. 1980. *Improving learning: an experiment in rural primary schools in Malaysia*, Evaluation in Education, 4:143-163.

Okpala, Promise ; Onocha, Charles, 1988. *Difficult physics topics in Nigerian secondary schools*, Physics Education, 23:168-72.

Pennick, John, E. ; Yager, R.E. ; Bonnstetter, Ronald, 1986. *Teachers make exemplary programs*, Ed. Lead., 44(2):12-20.

Pennington, F.W. 1985. "Needs Assessment in adult education", In T. Husén and T.N. Postlethwaite (editors.): *International Encyclopedia of Education.*

Plant, R. D. 1988. *A school investigation into Chernobyl fallout*, Physics Ed. 23(1):26-30.

Portelli, John, P. 1987. "Perspectives and imperatives on defining curriculum", *Journal of Curriculum and Supervision*, 2(4):354-67.

Pring, R. 1981. "Monitoring performance: reflections on the assessment of performance unit", in D. Lacy and D. Lawton (editors.), *Evaluation and Accountability*, London, Methuen.

Reid, W. 1987. "The function of SBCD: a cautionary note". In N. Sabar, et al (eds): *Partnership and autonomy*.

Rule, I.A.C. 1973. *A philosophical inquiry into the meaning(s) of curriculum*, Doctoral thesis at New York University.

Sabar, N. 1983. *School-based science curriculum development: myth or reality*, European Journal on Science Education 5(4):457-462.

Sabar, N, 1989. "Curriculum development, school-based", In T. Husén and T.N. Postlethwaite (editors.): *International Encyclopedia of Education*, Supplement no. 1.

Sabar, Naama ; Rudduck, Jean ; Reid, William, (editors). 1987. *Partnership and autonomy in school-based curriculum development*, Sheffield:University of Sheffield.

Schwab, J.J. 1971. "The practical: arts of the eclectic". In *School Review*, 79:493-542.

Schwab, J.J. 1983. "The practical 4: something for curriculum professors to do". In *Curriculum Inquiry*, 13(3):239-265.

Scottish Consultative Council on the Curriculum. 1989. *Curriculum Design for the Secondary Stages*, Dundee: Scottish Consultative Council on the Curriculum.

Secondary Science Curriculum Review, 1987. *Better science: a directory of resources*, London, Heineman.

Shipman, M. 1985. "Local educational authorities and the curriculum"; in P. Raggett and P. Weiner (editors); *Curriculum and assessment: some policy issues*, Oxford; Pergamon Press.

Silberstein, M. 1979. "Training teachers to implement general characteristics of the curriculum". In Tamir, P. ; Blum, A. ; Hofstein, A. (editors.), *Curriculum implementation and its relationship to its development*, Jerusalem, Hebrew University, Science Teaching Center.

Skilbeck, M. 1984. *School-based curriculum development*, London: Harper and Row.

Smith, O.B. ; Stanley, W.O. ; Shores, J.H. 1957. *Fundamentals of curriculum development*, rev. edn., New York: Harcourt, Brace.

Solomon, J. 1989. Science, technology and society as a curricular topic, In T. Husén and T.N. Postlethwaite (editors.): *International Encyclopedia of Education*.

Stromquist, Nelly P. 1986. "Decentralizing educational decision-making in Peru: intentions and reality", *International Journal on Educational Development*, 6 (1):47-60.

Stufflebeam, D. ; Foley, W.J. ; Gephart, W.J. ; Guba, E.J. ; Hammond, H.D. ; Merriman, H.O. ; Provus, M.M., 1971. *Educational evaluation and decision making*, Itasca,IL: Peacock.

Sutaria, M.C. 1990. "Teaching for maximum learning: the Philippines experience", *International Review of Education*, 36(2):243-50.

Taba, H. 1962. Curriculum Development: Theory and practice, New York: Harcourt, Brace and World.

Thomas, R.M. 1985a. "Supplementary curriculum programs", In T. Husén and T.N. Postlethwaite (editors.): *International Encyclopedia of Education.*

Thomas, R.M. 1985b. "Curriculum enrichment", In T. Husén ; T.N. Postlethwaite (editors.): *International Encyclopedia of Education.*

Tyler, R. W. 1950. *Basic principles of curriculum and instruction,* Chicago: University of Chicago Press.

Waddell, Sir James. 1978, *School Examinations,* London, HMSO.

Walker, D. 1976. *The IEA six subject survey: an empirical study of education in twenty-one countries,* Stockholm: Almqvist and Wiksell.

Walker, D.F. ; Schaffarzick, J. 1977. Comparing curricula, Rev. of Educational Res. 44(1): 83-111.

Willis, G. (ed.) 1978. *Qualitative evaluation,* Berkeley: McCutchan.

Wolfe, Michael, P. ; Howell, G.L.; Charland, J.A. 1989. *Energizing the school community: A research approach to practical school improvement,* Clearing House, 63(1):29-32.

Woodbury, M. 1979. *Selecting materials for instruction: issues and policies,* Littletown: Libraries Unlimited.

IIEP publications and documents

More than 650 titles on all aspects of educational planning have been published by the International Institute for Educational Planning. A comprehensive catalogue, giving details of their availability, includes research reports, case studies, seminar documents, training materials, occasional papers and reference books in the following subject categories:

Economics of education, costs and financing.

Manpower and employment.

Demographic studies.

The location of schools (school map) and sub-national planning.

Administration and management.

Curriculum development and evaluation.

Educational technology.

Primary, secondary and higher education.

Vocational and technical education.

Non-formal, out-of-school, adult and rural education.

Copies of the catalogue may be obtained from the IIEP on request.